Critical Guides to French T

D1461683

61 Thomas's *Tristan* and the *Folie Tristan d'Oxford*

Critical Guides to French Texts

EDITED BY ROGER LITTLE, WOLFGANG VAN EMDEN, DAVID WILLIAMS

Thomas's Tristan and the Folie Tristan d'Oxford

Geoffrey N. Bromiley

Lecturer in French
University of Durham

Grant & Cutler Ltd
1986

© Grant & Cutler Ltd
1986

Library of Congress Cataloging-in-Publication Data

Bromiley, Geoffrey N., 1942-
  Thomas's Tristan and the Folie Tristan d'Oxford.

  (Critical guides to French texts: 61)
  Bibliography: p.
  1. Tristan (Legendary character)—Romances—History and criticism. 2.
Romances—History and criticism. 3. French poetry—To 1500—History and
criticism. 4. Thomas (Anglo-Norman poet). Roman de Tristan. 5. Folie
Tristan d'Oxford. I. Title. II. Series.
PQ1543.B76 1986   841'.1'09351   86-25650
ISBN 0-7293-0257-1

I.S.B.N. 84-599-1694-4

DEPÓSITO LEGAL: 2.051 - 1986

Printed in Spain by
Artes Gráficas Soler, S.A., Valencia
for
GRANT & CUTLER LTD
55-57, GREAT MARLBOROUGH STREET, LONDON W1V 2AY
and
27, SOUTH MAIN STREET, WOLFEBORO, NH 03894-2069, USA

Contents

Preface

Both Thomas's *Tristan* and the *Folie Tristan d'Oxford* have been edited on a number of occasions. All references to Thomas's text are to the *Textes littéraires français* edition by Bartina H. Wind (Bibliography, *5*). For the *Folie Tristan d'Oxford* I have employed, for reasons of accessibility alone, the edition by J.C. Payen (Bibliography, *51*): the edition of E. Hoepffner (Bibliography, *50*) is more scholarly.

The customary abbreviations will be employed for the Thomas manuscript fragments:

> D. (Douce)
> Sn.[1], Sn.[2] (Sneyd)
> T.[1], T.[2] (Turin)
> Str.[1], Str.[2], Str.[3] (Strasbourg)
> C. (Cambridge)

The conventional sigla will be employed for the various versions of the Tristan legend (full references are given in the Bibliography).

T	Thomas
G	Gottfried von Strassburg, edited by Ranke
E	*Sir Tristrem*, edited by Kölbing
S	*Tristrams Saga ok Isöndar*, edited by Kölbing
B	*The Romance of Tristran by Beroul*, edited by Ewert
O	Eilhart von Oberg, edited by Buschinger
Fo	*Folie Tristan d'Oxford*

Italicized numbers in brackets, followed where appropriate by a page reference, refer to the numbered items in the Bibliography at the end of this volume.

1. Introduction

In general, time has dealt harshly with the medieval Tristan texts, and it has certainly not spared the version written by Thomas (*T*). Of the complete romance, only fragments, eight in number, have been known, all concerned with events in the second half of the story. The Douce (D.) and Sneyd manuscripts (Sn.[1], Sn.[2]) are in Oxford and the Cambridge fragment in the Cambridge University Library. But the whereabouts of the two Turin fragments (T.[1], T.[2]), published by Novati in 1887 (see *3*), is now a mystery and the three Strasbourg fragments (Str.[1], Str.[2], Str.[3]), which Francisque Michel edited in 1835 (see *2*), are irretrievably lost, destroyed by fire in 1870.

In another respect, however, Thomas's romance has been relatively fortunate. The work of Beroul, the other major twelfth-century French version, survives only as a single fragment; it inspired no imitators, so far as we know, and the precise contents of the complete poem must accordingly remain uncertain.[1] But not long after Thomas's work was produced, it was taken up by other writers in other countries, and we now have three major derivative versions, the Middle High German romance of Gottfried von Strassburg (*G*), the Norse *Saga* (*S*) and the Middle English *Sir Tristrem* (*E*). None of these derivative versions is in any sense a translation. Gottfried — who probably brought his work to its present, unfinished form round about 1210 — claims in his prologue to be following the work of Thomas, the only true authority. But he also admits there to knowledge of other versions and there is no doubt that in the main body of his text he has introduced modifications to the story the French poet gave him. Similarly, Brother Robert, the author of *Tristrams saga ok Isöndar* (written a little later, in 1226), was clearly prepared to depart from what lay before him.

[1] For information on Beroul's text, see Peter S. Noble, *Beroul's 'Tristan' and the 'Folie de Berne'* (London, Grant and Cutler, 1982).

But above all he condensed: some minor episodes are excised, many lengthy speeches are abbreviated and passages of psychological analysis are suppressed. The author of the Middle English version, a late thirteenth-century romance with a complicated stanza form, also drastically cut Thomas's poem. No major episode is actually omitted, but long passages of psychological debate in particular are once again eliminated. Another generally acknowledged derivative of Thomas's romance is the episodic poem, the *Folie Tristan d'Oxford* (*Fo*). As a French poem it merits special attention and a later chapter in this study is devoted exclusively to it.

In spite of the changes introduced by their respective authors, these derivative versions do enable us to reconstruct with some confidence the main lines at least of Thomas's original narrative. They did in fact form the basis of the reconstruction undertaken by Joseph Bédier in the volume he published in 1902 (see *1*, vol. I). But Bédier did more than simply re-create Thomas's romance. He produced a second volume in 1905 (see *1*, vol. II) in which he examined the episodes preserved in Thomas's poem, in Beroul's romance (*B*), in the Middle High German work by Eilhart (*0*) and in the thirteenth-century French Prose Romance. He reached the conclusion that at the head of the whole Tristan tradition there existed an archetype, a single source from which all the known Tristan poems are ultimately derived, the composition of one man at the beginning of the twelfth century; he then set out to reconstruct this lost primitive romance. Both of Bédier's reconstructions must be treated with considerable caution. Bédier himself admitted, quite rightly, that his reconstruction of Thomas's poem was not purely mechanical but was also a matter of taste (see *1*, vol. I, pp.vi-vii), and it is extremely doubtful whether the original Tristan poem — if, indeed, there ever was one — can be reproduced in anything like the detail the French critic supposed. Although I shall naturally be concentrating my attention in this study on those sections of Thomas's romance that remain, some knowledge of the story up to the first surviving fragment is definitely desirable. Professor Wind has supplied a useful, if brief summary of events in her editions (see *4*, pp.57-59, *5*, pp.23-27). I propose now to discuss a number of episodes from the early and central part of the story in the form suggested by Bédier's reconstruction, in order to aid understanding of the work's content and also in order to give some preliminary indication of Thomas's working methods.

Thomas begins his story with a tragic love story involving Tristan's parents, before he turns to his hero and the tragic love story proper. Brought to Cornwall, Tristan reveals his identity to King Mark, his uncle, defeats the Morholt in battle, but suffers a poisoned wound in combat. He is placed in a boat and is carried to Ireland, where he has his wound healed by the queen of the country and where he meets the queen's daughter Iseut. When Tristan is completely recovered, he takes ship and returns to Tintagel.

The story has now to make a new start. In the version Thomas chooses to modify and which is probably best preserved at this point by *0*, the Cornish barons, jealous of Tristan's ascendancy over Mark, urge the king to marry. On the day Mark has to respond to their request, a swallow enters the castle and drops a blond hair. Mark then tells the company that he will marry the lady from whom the hair came and Tristan offers to seek this lady, wherever and whoever she may be. He sets sail with a number of companions and they are carried by a storm to Ireland. When Thomas described Tristan's first journey to Ireland, in search of a cure for his wound, he seems to have tried to eliminate the marvellous element he inherited from his source, but in the end he failed. Now, he tries again, and on this occasion, he is more successful. First, Thomas has Tristan sing the praises of the Irish princess on his return to Cornwall: this surely represents an attempt to effect a smooth transition between episodes. He then goes on to attack the story with the swallow; Gottfried, probably echoing Thomas, writes:

> weiz got, hie spellet sich der leich,
> hie lispet daz mære. (*G*,ll.8614-15)

('I do think this section of the story is incredible, it really sounds like nonsense').

In *T*, we have no swallow and no blond hair, but instead a number of claims and counterclaims. The Cornish barons argue that it is now time for Mark to marry in order to have sons who would safeguard the realm, but the king retorts he has already acknowledged Tristan as his heir. When all the nobles in concert urge Mark to take a wife, the king replies that the person chosen must be his equal in rank and worthy of him in every way. After a delay, the Cornish barons announce to Mark that the daughter of the Queen of Ireland would be an admirable choice. They point out the political advantages of such a match and go on to suggest that Tristan, since he is familiar with Ireland and has met Iseut already, is the natural choice of envoy, knowing full well that as the slayer of the Morholt, the Irish giant, he is unlikely to return alive. Tristan makes preparations for his journey which is no *voyage à l'aventure* but one with an already determined and dangerous goal: he sets sail straight for Ireland. In place of a tale whose progress is governed by the intervention of the *merveilleux*, Thomas has introduced a series of rational and psychologically credible developments.

In the course of his second stay in Ireland, Tristan eventually wins Iseut for King Mark. His mission accomplished, he then sets sail for Cornwall. Thomas has now come to a fixed event in the narrative; he must include at this point an episode which tells of the drinking of the love-potion on board ship. The philtre has been prepared by the Queen of Ireland, is intended for Mark and his bride and has been entrusted to Brengain, Iseut's lady-in-waiting and confidante. As the voyage goes on, the heat becomes oppressive. Tristan asks for wine and first he, and then Iseut, drink from the potion inadvertently handed over to them. One can be fairly certain that in the original romance there followed a series of extended monologues and dialogues, as Iseut and Tristan come to confess their love for each other and consummate their relationship. It is the significance of this episode in *T* which is of particular interest. In the common source, the potion was almost certainly limited in power (it is limited to three years in *B*, to four years in *O*) and only after this set period of time are the lovers able to contemplate separation. Thomas wishes to attenuate the magical properties associated with the potion, much as he eliminated the marvellous element he found in the swallow's hair story, and he seems to have tried to elevate the philtre to the level of a symbol. There is no indication that in his version the potion ever ceased to function and a parallel is suggested between the permanence of the potion's effect and the enduring nature of the love. That is what Thomas seems to have attempted, without being completely successful: the potion does not altogether lose its material existence, as one might henceforth expect, for Thomas has Mark drink what remains of it on his wedding night. Nevertheless, Thomas has given us to understand that he may well be concerned with a different kind of love from that presented by earlier strata of the legend and by other extant texts. In fact, Thomas's concern with a different kind of love inspired the traditional (if disputed) division of the Tristan texts into the *version commune* and the *version courtoise*: the *version commune* group has *B* and *O* as its main members, whilst the second group is represented by *T* and its derivatives, texts imbued with the notions of *fine amor*, of courtly love.

Once Tristan and Iseut reach Cornwall, there begins a series of adventures characterized by intrigue and deception, by ruse and counter-ruse, as the lovers strive to keep the love secret. Thomas passes over a number of scenes probably supplied by his source and preserved by Beroul, in which the lovers were condemned to death but then escaped to the forest: one assumes that the barbarity of these scenes was felt to be jarring and so caused their exclusion. A passage describing the lovers' period of exile away from court is not now essential to Thomas's recast account, but he decides to provide his own version of the life in the forest, unable to resist the possibilities of the scene.

But how is he to get Tristan and Iseut to the forest? Typically in *T*, their departure from court is not provoked by any outside agent but by Mark's psychological state. The king is very soon beset by suspicion and jealousy, and eventually, unwilling to tolerate the situation any more, he has the lovers leave. In the story which Thomas took over, and which Beroul largely continued, the lovers must endure a life of hardship in the forest and are for ever on the move, in constant fear of detection and death. Thomas's lovers, however, lead a life of ease, nourished by their devotion to each other; they are not nomads, but live in a cave called by Gottfried, and perhaps by Thomas before him, 'la fossiure a la gent amant' (*G*, 1.17224). They have the dog, Husdent, with them, and, as in Beroul's poem and the French Prose Romance, the dog was probably taught in *T* to catch his prey without yielding to the temptation to bark. There is no desperate necessity in *T* for the dog to hunt silently: Tristan and Iseut have gladly accepted their exile and do not fear recapture, but presumably Thomas was reluctant to abandon such an appealing story.

In due course of time, the lovers' whereabouts are discovered. King Mark is brought to the scene by his huntsmen and, seeing a sword set between the lovers, decides that they are not lusting for each other. Of the derivative versions, Gottfried's is the most complex and it is probably developing or even largely reproducing Thomas's account: Mark passes through several psychological states until finally Love (*Minne*) convinces him of the couple's innocence. Mark then calls Tristan and Iseut back to court. One wonders how Thomas explained the apparently ready response of the lovers to the king's summons and their immediate abandonment of their earthly paradise. But if the narrative is to continue, a return to court is necessary, and it is an incident at the court that will form the matter of the first surviving fragment.

Thomas names himself twice in the fragments that remain, referring to himself as 'Thomas' at 1.862 of D. and 'Tumas', possibly a form of Welsh provenance (see *25*, p.495), at 1.820 of Sn.[2]. Attempts have been made to identify our writer with other known writers of the same name, but no identification has so far gained any kind of general acceptance. In particular, attempts to suggest that the Tristan writer was the Thomas who wrote the *Romance of Horn* or Thomas of Kent, the putative author of the *Roman de toute chevalerie*, have failed to convince (on this matter, see *37*, p.49, *48*, pp.1130-31). The writers of derivative versions have done nothing to help matters in this respect. Gottfried von Strassburg names the author of his main source in his prologue as 'Thomas von Britanje' (*G*, 1.150), but it may well be that he was seeking to lend to Thomas a knowledge of things

Celtic that really belonged to a source of Thomas (see *1*, vol.II, pp.38-39). The author of *S* does not mention Thomas at all, but the author of *E* claims in the first line of his version (if we accept the text) to have met Thomas at 'Erceldoune', Earlston in Berwickshire! This does seem to represent a deliberate attempt on the part of the English author — whoever he was! — to associate the Thomas of the French romance with the thirteenth-century Border poet, Thomas of Erceldoune or Thomas the Rhymer.

But did Thomas himself have an English connection? Early critical opinion took his English provenance almost for granted and even in more recent times scholars have regularly termed him Thomas d'Angleterre, whether they believed in his insular origins or not. But evidence to support this appellation is scanty. There are certainly Anglo-Norman features, traces of the literary language employed in England, in the fragments that remain. Bartina H. Wind, after her consideration of the poet's language in her 1950 edition of the text, suggests that Thomas was French rather than English and enunciates a very cautious conclusion: 'Thomas a écrit dans le français littéraire de la cour des Plantagenets, mais il a connu les particularités du parler anglo-normand, qu'elles lui aient appartenu en propre ou non. Il a voulu les écarter de son œuvre de propos déliberé: quelques-unes lui ont cependant échappé' (*4*, p.47). Another element in the text which to some has suggested the English origins of the author is the eulogistic description of London included in the Douce fragment:

> Lundres est mult riche cité,
> Meliur n'ad en cristienté,
> Plus vaillante ne melz aisie
> Melz guarnie de gent preisie.
> Mult aiment largesce e honur,
> Cunteinent sei par grant baldur.
> Le recovrer est de Engleterre:
> Avant d'iloc ne l'estuet querre.
> Al pé del mur li curt Tamise;
> Par le vent la marchandise
> De tutes les teres qui sunt

Un marcheant cristien vunt.
Li hume i sunt de grant engin.

(D., ll.1379-91)

Descriptions of towns are found elsewhere — the description of
Escavalon supplied by Chrétien de Troyes in the *Conte du Graal*
comes to mind — and other writers, notably Wace in the *Roman
de Brut*, have indicated the importance of London in this period.
But in praising London and its inhabitants, Thomas has
introduced a development hardly called for by the strict
exigencies of the narrative, and on the strength of this passage
alone one might fairly reasonably suppose that Thomas was
living in England and writing for an English audience. To
suggest that Thomas was himself English is another matter
—Wace, for whom London was an important bishopric, came
after all from Jersey! The notion of an English audience is
reinforced somewhat if the derivative versions are considered.
G, *S* and *E* concur in indicating that Thomas made King Mark
the ruler, not merely of Cornwall as he was traditionally, but
also of England. Gottfried was thus able, towards the beginning
of his work (ll.427-53), to sing the praises of Mark and England
in a passage which he may have taken from Thomas, who, in
turn, may have been inspired by Wace (see *1*, vol. I, p.5, note 1).
But is it possible to be any more precise as regards the audience
for which Thomas was writing? The call, 'Seignurs' (D., l.835),
is a commonplace and cannot be held to support the view that
the work was produced for the court nobility. Nevertheless, the
complexity of the dialectic in the surviving fragments does
suggest that Thomas had some kind of sophisticated élite in
mind. Certainly Thomas could have been writing for the court,
but it must be recognized that in spite of a number of ingenious
articles, notably by Legge and Lejeune (see *36* and *38*), no firm
evidence has been adduced which would directly associate either
Henry II or Eleanor of Aquitaine with the work. A determined
effort has also been made to connect Thomas's romance with
the court of the earldom of Gloucester (see *25*). Perhaps above
all, though, we need to remind ourselves that no dedication, if
there ever was one, now survives and that, as Wind suggests,

caution should be the order of the day: 'Méfions-nous des conclusions qui vont au-delà de ce que justifie une documentation précise' (*48*, p.1133).

There is perhaps more evidence in the text to indicate Thomas's social status, for within the extant fragments there are passages which possibly suggest that Thomas was a member of the clergy. When Novati published the Turin fragments in 1887, he drew attention to three particular passages which, in his view, had the mark of the ecclesiastic, since they seemed to him to reveal an ignorance of the nature of women and of the ways of the world in general (see *3*, p.403, note 3): the passages in question are ll.287-91 and 369-84 of Sn.[1], and ll.1323-35 of D. Bédier rejected Novati's supposition (see *1*, vol. II, pp.43-45), arguing with some justification that he had misinterpreted the passages, and then arguing, rather more dangerously, that a reconstruction of Thomas's complete text suggested a poet with a much wider range of preoccupations than those supposed by Novati. The whole question has been re-opened by Jonin in an important chapter of *Les Personnages féminins dans les romans français de Tristan* (*31*, pp.373-450). In a close examination of the text, he points to many places where the influence of religious literature can be seen and reaches the following conclusions: 'A la plupart des problèmes laissés insolubles par l'interprétation courtoise, la clergie de Thomas apporte une réponse' (*31*, p.450). Thomas was undoubtedly a 'clerc', a man who had been through the schools, but whether one can go further and declare that Thomas was necessarily a practising priest is quite another question: the kind of religious knowledge deployed by the author would not have been the exclusive preserve of a particular class of men, certainly not in the medieval period. If the author were a man of the cloth, we would somehow need to come to terms with the fact that his choice of subject-matter, on the surface at least, is rather surprising.

The final problem that needs to be discussed here, the dating of Thomas's romance, is predictably just as much a matter of debate as the question of authorship. The linguistic evidence, touched upon already when the question of Thomas's English origins was mentioned, does not seem susceptible of any firm conclusion. There are features which may be termed archaic and which suggest an 'early' date, but these features may easily reflect Anglo-Norman linguistic conservatism (see *4*, p.39).

If we choose to employ literary criteria in an attempt to date the text, we are pleasantly surprised to be able to begin with a certainty, or at least an undisputed claim, namely that Thomas's work has been influenced by Wace's *Roman de Brut* (see *41*, pp.72-97). What is more, Wace obligingly tells us that he finished his story in 1155. Thus, the earliest date, the *terminus a quo*, for *T* must be 1155 and the latest date, the *terminus ad quem*, 1210, the accepted date of the derivative version of Gottfried von Strassburg. But after this we are once again in the realms of speculation. One form of investigation that has been undertaken has been into the relationship of *T* to other texts, notably to the romances of Chrétien de Troyes. To Chrétien, the Tristan legend was apparently something of an obsession: at the beginning of *Cligés*, amongst his other compositions, he mentions a work 'Del roi Marc et d'Ysalt la blonde', which, so its description suggests, was probably a shortish poem rather than a fully-fledged Tristan romance. But the influence of the legend can be seen elsewhere in Chrétien's work. The belief that there was a direct association between *T* and the *Chevalier de la Charrette* is now long since discarded (see *1*, vol. II, pp.47-53), but it is plain that there did exist a relationship between *T* and *Cligés*. There is an extended pun in *Cligés* made on the words *la mer*, *l'amer* and *amer* and Gottfried — and therefore probably Thomas — develops the same conceit (*G*, ll.11956-12028) as the lovers, having drunk the potion, confess their love for each other on the boat bearing them to Cornwall. But *T* may not necessarily be following *Cligés* or *Cligés T*: Thomas himself indicates the variety of the Tristan material (see D., ll.835 ff.) and both he and Chrétien could have absorbed the pun from the general corpus of material that was available. Moreover, it has been shown that the pun has a very long ancestry (see *28*). Nevertheless, if the pun was borrowed by Thomas or Chrétien, the existence of other associations between the two romances does suggest that one writer borrowed from the other, rather than from a different source altogether. These associations have been thoroughly investigated by Anthime Fourrier (see *20*). He has indicated that Chrétien knew, as well as other Tristan material, the version of Thomas in particular, that improbabilities in *Cligés* can be understood if one sees Chrétien as a writer attempting to present the elements of *T* in a different order and that *Cligés* is above all a response to Thomas's romance. He claims in essence that 'Chrétien de Troyes a composé *Cligés* sous l'influence immédiate du grand poème de Thomas et dans le dessein de rivaliser avec lui' (*20*, p.154). More recently, Lucie Polak has pointed out analogies between *Cligés* and the Tristan story and between *Cligés* and Thomas's version in particular. She has, moreover, indicated precise passages where Chrétien may be echoing passages in *T* (see *44*, pp.50-69).

Fourrier also attempted to determine the date of Thomas by employing criteria which might be termed 'historical' or 'cultural'. He submitted the episodes in Thomas's version to detailed analysis and suggested that Thomas adapted the story to the taste of his time and to the prevailing pattern of Anglo-Irish relationships. He concluded that Thomas must have begun his work about the middle of 1172 and finished it two or three years later (see *20*, pp.108-09). But even as he formulated this conclusion, Fourrier had to admit that historical events may not necessarily have found parallels in the modifications introduced by the poet. Moreover, many of his arguments are, once again, inevitably based on the shaky evidence afforded by the reconstruction and certain of these arguments have been opposed, notably by Legge, who rather sadly pronounces: 'It is therefore impossible to date this romance by historical allusion' (*37*, p.49). In the past, Legge had not herself shied away from attempting to date the text using related criteria, the supposed, special relationship enjoyed by Thomas with the court of Eleanor of Aquitaine: she suggested 1158 as a possible date (see *36*). Using much the same criteria and in particular the peregrinations of the Plantagenets, Rita Lejeune has opted for a date between 1154 and 1158 (see *38*). But one must insist once again that the presence of Thomas at the court of Eleanor, however likely this may seem in certain quarters, is just not proven. Equally unsatisfactory have been attempts to date T through the coat-of-arms granted to Tristan before his battle with the Morholt. For since the derivative versions disagree as to the precise nature of Tristan's arms, it seems rash to suggest a date for the romance on this kind of evidence.[2] Indeed, none of the evidence that has so far been assembled provides us with anything like a precise date for Thomas's poem. Before *Cligés*, one might say with Fourrier and Polak, but when was *Cligés* written? Luttrell's consideration of the works of Chrétien de Troyes suggests a date in the mid-1180s (see *39*, pp.33-46), but this is a decade later than Fourrier's proposal of 1176-77. All in all, one can only sympathize with Wind who, in her 1950 edition, opted for the writing of the *Tristan* between 1180 and 1190 (see *4*, p.16), but who then, in her 1960 edition, suggested the period 1150-60 (see *5*, p.17)! Here, she sounds once again the appropriate cautionary note: 'Mais il faut sans doute renoncer à chercher des précisions que nous ne pouvons obtenir; toutes les hypothèses sont invérifiables; la question reste ouverte'.

These introductory remarks have not brought us very far. Very little can be known for certain of the identity of Thomas, of his provenance, his position in life or the date when he produced his Tristan poem. Speculation on these matters does, of course, have its own interest, and some scholars must have reached the right conclusions. But, because of the paucity of the evidence, we shall never be sure which conclusions were in fact the correct ones. Still, to realize that some things will never be knowable does represent progress of a kind, and this is certainly true if we go on to recognize that what remains of Thomas's text must become the centre of our preoccupations. Naturally, we need also to know something of the works directly derived from Thomas in order to have some appreciation of what the original, full romance may have contained and to have some general insight into our poet's working methods. At the same time, we must not allow our understanding of Thomas's poem to be

[2] On this matter and for information as to the relevant literature, see Gerard J. Brault, *Early Blazon: heraldic terminology in the twelfth and thirteenth centuries with special reference to Arthurian literature* (Oxford, Clarendon Press, 1972), pp.19-21.

governed by the derivative versions: when a work is rewritten in a different language for a different audience it inevitably takes on a new flavour and comes to contain new points of emphasis. Given the fragmentary state of the surviving romance our understanding will inevitably remain incomplete, but at least we shall have tried to give an authentic response, unbiased as far as possible by potentially misleading external factors, to what Thomas actually wrote.

2. Narrative Invention

'Même dans les menus détails s'exerce
l'esprit logique et méticuleux de Thomas'
(A. Fourrier)

Eilhart's account of the deaths of the lovers and events immediately preceding runs as follows.

Kehenis (Thomas's Kaherdin) is in love with Gariole, the wife of Nampetenis. Tristan has already attempted to further his friend's affair and he now rides with Kehenis to the castle of Nampetenis, at a time when they know he will be absent. Gariole welcomes Kehenis, but Tristan remains outside and amuses himself throwing twigs at a wall. When Nampetenis returns, he sees the twigs and other indications, correctly assumes that Tristan and Kehenis have just been there, pursues them, kills Kehenis and wounds Tristan with a poisoned lance. Realizing that only the queen can save him, Tristan sends his host (his 'wirt') to bring Iseut back to Brittany, instructing him to have a white sail set if she is on the ship with him, a black one if she has remained behind; Tristan also instructs his host to have his daughter watch the sea so that she can tell him the colour of the sail when the ship appears. Tristan's wife, in some undisclosed way, learns something of these plans, but precisely what remains obscure. When the daughter of the host sees the ship returning, she tells the second Iseut of the coming of the vessel and of its white sail, but Iseut tells her husband the sail is not white and Tristan's death then follows. When Queen Iseut reaches the shore, she hears of her lover's death and expires as well.

This is not a very accomplished tale: the reasons why the second Iseut behaves as she does remain very much a mystery, the introduction of two new characters, in the form of the host and his daughter, is not very happy and the affair between Kehenis and Gariole strikes a somewhat sordid note.

Perhaps deliberately, immediately before Thomas embarks upon his own, individual account of events leading up to the lovers' deaths, he intervenes personally and introduces a passage which amounts to a kind of artistic credo, a defence not only of what he is proposing to do, but also of what he has done already:

> Seignurs, cest cunte est mult divers,
> E pur ço l'uni par mes vers
> E di en tant cum est mester
> E le surplus voil relesser.
> Ne vol pas trop en uni dire.
>
> (D., ll.835-39)

We learn that there was a Tristan story ('cest cunte'), made up of extremely disparate material ('mult divers'): this presumably means that there were different versions of roughly the same incidents, and not that there was one story with internal contradictions. As Kelly has explained (*32*), Thomas has gathered together ('uni') this material for his own version, selected certain parts of it and rejected other, non-essential parts (ll.837-39). He then goes on to say that at this point in the tale a number of divergent accounts exist: 'Ici diverse la matyre' (l.840). He has heard oral accounts and also knows written accounts, produced by the performers of the oral versions. Like others, so he claims (l.853), he proposes to reject a version, apparently telling a story similar to that found in *O*, in which Kaherdin loved the wife of a dwarf, was killed by the dwarf, who then treacherously also wounded Tristan. Further, he rejects the version which claimed that Governal was the messenger sent by Tristan to summon Queen Iseut to his side. This, Thomas claims — and now he speaks alone — offends the rules of logic:

> Thomas iço granter ne volt,
> E si volt par raisun mustrer
> Qu'iço ne put pas esteer.
>
> (D., ll.862-64)

Pointing out that Governal was a known ally of Tristan and
Iseut, was hated by Mark and would be instantly recognizable at
court, he dismisses those who peddle such improbabilities:

> Il sunt del cunte forsveié
> E de la verur esluingné.
>
> (D., ll.879-80)

In fact, the version Thomas attacks is nothing like as implausible
as he claims: Tristan himself has already visited the court in
disguise, has shown himself to the 'baruns' and 'serjanz'
mentioned in 1.873 and has escaped detection by his enemies
(D., ll.535 ff.). All the same, Thomas does take *raisun* as his
watchword and, having brought together his material, discards
what he considers improbable.

Near the start of the passage Thomas invokes the authority of
a certain Breri:

> Ky solt les gestes e les cuntes
> De tuz les reis, de tuz les cuntes
> Ki orent esté en Bretaingne.
>
> (D., ll.849-51)

Thomas believed Breri to be a real person and, indeed, he may
be identified with the figure described by Gerald of Wales in his
Descriptio Cambriae as 'famosus ille fabulator Bledhericus qui
tempora nostra paulo praevenit' ('the famous storyteller...who
lived a little before our time'), the Welsh noble, Bledri son of
Cadifor (born circa 1069, died circa 1133). He seems to have
been pro-Norman and to have served the invaders in the role of
latimer, a professional interpreter, and he may in fact have acted
in this capacity for Henry I, in Pembroke and Carmarthen,
when the king came to Wales. Before this period, he seems to
have visited Poitiers and to have told the story of Perceval to the
count of Poitou, William IX of Aquitaine, the famous
troubadour (see *17*, pp.10-12, *23* and *25*, pp.482-84). It is quite
common for a medieval author to appeal to an authority in
order to justify his own particular version, but what is slightly

unusual here is that there is no suggestion Breri ever *wrote* a word himself: he was a *conteur*, relating the story in a way Thomas claims to approve. Thomas never actually states that he is reproducing the tale as Breri told it and I suspect that, as is frequently the case, this appeal to an authority conceals a personal invention. Indeed, Thomas closes the passage expressing pride in his own achievement and confidence that his version will be recognized as superior to that of his competitors:

> Tengent le lur e jo le men:
> La raisun s'i pruvera ben!
>
> (D., ll.883-84)

So, Thomas was obviously dissatisfied with the account of the lovers' deaths which he inherited, an account by no means identical to that preserved in Eilhart, for the German version itself contains features which must represent a remodelling of the received data. But, whatever was in the original story, Eilhart's version is incoherent, while Thomas's version proves to be decidedly more logical. Our author's concern for rationality, noticed already in his reworking of the episode concerning the swallow and the quest for the owner of the golden hair, is apparent here as well.

Thomas achieves a logical account, first by making the reasons for the behaviour of Tristan's wife much more plain. We are told how she learns of the significance of the colour of the sail; she is listening in an adjacent room when Tristan gives the messenger to the queen his instructions:

> Ysolt estoit suz la parei,
> Les diz Tristran escute e ot,
> Ben ad entendu chacun mot.
>
> (D., ll.1336-38)

Her marriage unconsummated, Iseut is undoubtedly motivated by a desire for revenge (D., ll.1346-49) and when she misinforms Tristan as to the colour of the sail, it is plain she is acting with malice aforethought: 'Purpensee de grant engin' (D., l.1741).

Thomas's choice of messenger to the queen is also eminently reasonable. Avoiding Eilhart's expedient of inventing new characters at this point, Thomas has Tristan send Kaherdin, who in his version is still very much alive. Thomas's concern for narrative logic.is also seen in the way in which he inserts a minor detail. A storm strikes the queen's ship as it heads for Brittany and smashes the small boat, which we know the vessel carries since it has had a part to play already in the course of this mission (see D., ll.1375-76, 1523-29):

> Lur batel orent en mer mis,
> Car pres furent de leur païs;
> A mal eür l'unt ublié:
> Une wage l'ad despescé.
>
> (D., ll.1605-08)

A little later, Iseut's ship is becalmed, within sight of land, but she and her companions are unable to row to shore, as we might reasonably once have anticipated, for 'lur batel n'unt il mie' (D., l.1717). Thomas thus seeks, through the care with which he presents this detail, to maintain the credibility of his account.

Thomas includes other material with the refinement of the tale as his aim, the same impulse which seems to have led to his omitting a number of scenes concerned with the lovers' condemnation and escape to the forest. In his version, Tristan is no longer Kaherdin's accomplice in adultery, but receives his poisoned wound while trying to help a wronged lover whose lady has been taken from him. Acting as he does out of pity for a fellow knight, Tristan's motives are impeccable (D., ll.1010-16). Other elements in the narrative have other ends in view. Thomas introduces the description of London (D., ll.1379-91) which, though scarcely sustained, does increase the sense of occasion when Kaherdin arrives in the city bearing the crucial message from Tristan and Iseut. Then, the storm which strikes Iseut's ship as her goal is almost in sight (D., ll.1592 ff.) has as its most immediate purpose a raising of tension at a time when it seems possible that all may be well.

It is difficult to know how much of this material was created by Thomas himself, but he has certainly engaged in a considerable remodelling of the last scenes of the story. His willingness to produce an individual account makes, on one occasion at least, the invention of an episode well-nigh essential. As I have remarked already, there is no indication, either in the surviving fragments or in the derivative versions, that in Thomas's poem the love potion ever lost its power. But a problem consequently presents itself at one stage in the story. In *B* and *O*, the potion ceases to function with its original compulsive force and the lovers, freed from its control, are able to separate. In order to use material he has available, Thomas also needs to bring about the separation of the lovers: this he achieves by inventing the *Verger* episode preserved in the Cambridge fragment. Not that he creates the episode out of nothing: Fourrier quite rightly describes it as 'une combinaison d'éléments empruntés à divers épisodes du modèle' (*20*, p.88). Indeed, there are obvious parallels between the accounts of the lovers' separation in *B* and *O* (which presumably continue in part the account of the common source) and the account here in *T*, but perhaps a crucial inspiration has been the Separating Sword episode (see *1*, vol.II, pp.256-57). What Thomas seems to have done is to develop the potential of this episode in his source and to confirm in his own, invented episode what remained a false hypothesis in his original material. In Beroul's version of the incident (ll.1774-2132), Iseut wakes from a dream and cries out, disturbing Tristan. He reaches for his sword and then realizes his own sword has been replaced by another. Iseut, for her part, sees that her ring has gone. The lovers, their reaction coloured by an awareness of guilt, then assume that the king wishes to harm them and has gone for men in order to effect their capture. In Eilhart's version (ll.4581-4701), the lovers awake, see the king's glove and his sword and think they are in mortal danger; Mark, so they believe, has only stayed his hand because he felt it unseemly to kill them while they were asleep. In both these versions, and presumably also in the common source shared by *B*, *O* and *T*, the lovers are wrong to suppose their lives are in danger. But in Thomas's new episode, the lovers' lives are genuinely under threat, for after Mark finds them asleep

together he goes in search of men who will witness their adultery
and thereby justify his putting them to death:

> 'En cel palais la sus irai,
> De mes barons i amerrai:
> Verront com les avon trovez;
> Ardoir les frai, quant ert pruvez.'
>
> (C., ll.10-13)

What never happened in the Separating Sword incident of
Thomas's source actually comes about in his invented episode.
Mark might reasonably have reacted in another way to the scene
in the garden: that his reaction took the particular form it did
may well be because Thomas turned a hypothesis of his source
into a reality (see *16*, especially pp.746-49).

In spite of our author's considerable ingenuity, the *Verger*
episode is not really a success. The handing over of a ring as a
pledge of love and the granting of a kiss as confirmation of that
love could not be more conventional, and Iseut does little more
in this scene than echo the sentiments voiced by Tristan. The
dwarf who brought the king to the garden plays a strangely
vague role, so much so that in *G* he is deemed dispensable and
does not appear at all. And why does Tristan withdraw
completely and anticipate a long period of separation from
Iseut? Why, with the memory of the idyll in the forest fresh in
his mind, does Tristan fail to take Iseut with him? But escaping
together would frustrate the whole purpose of the episode!
Drawing on disparate material from other scenes in the legend,
Thomas has brought about the situation he finds at the end of
the separation scene in his source: Iseut will now be living with
her husband and her lover can embark upon his adventures in
Brittany.

Another invention of Thomas is the *Salle aux images* episode
(T.[1]). Of course, the scene does contain features found in other
texts. Although the beginning of the scene is missing, the
evidence of *S* indicates that Thomas retold here the story of
Elaine's abduction by a giant, as found in Wace, and attributed
to the giant the building of the mysterious subterranean

chamber. Further, Thomas may have been inspired by Wace to choose the Mont Saint Michel (mentioned in *S*) as the setting for his episode and he may also have remembered Wace's tale of Locrinus and Estrildis. Critics have pointed to the alabaster chamber in the *Roman de Troie* and to the chapel in the forest where Guilliadun is hidden in Marie de France's *Eliduc*. Classical reminiscences, the Pygmalion tale and the story of the Roman youth who married the statue of Venus, have also been detected. (On all these parallels, see *1*, vol. I, pp.397-99, *20*, p.97 and especially *43*.) But out of his sources Thomas has certainly created something distinctive.

What must have been unusual in the complete romance, so far as one can judge from *S* and *E*, is the inclusion of precise description: a place is described, as are images of people, the statues of Iseut and Brengain. Little of this survives, except the brief sketch of Iseut in ll.35-38:

> Regarde en la main Ysodt,
> L'anel d'or doner li volt,
> Vait la chere e le senblant
> Qu'au departir fait son amant.

The statues have obviously to be presented as precise likenesses if they are to help Tristan in the purposes for which they were created. The image of Iseut is for him a substitute for the absent queen, to be embraced — rather dubiously — as if it were a real person: 'Molt la baise quant est haitez' (T.[1], l.5). At the same time, the statue is a reminder of the queen, bringing back memories of the past they shared together and, in particular, of the moment of parting in the *Verger*, the occasion they last saw each other. The ring Tristan sees on the finger of the statue recalls the real Iseut and the declaration of loyalty she made in the garden, just as the genuine ring itself, when it falls from Tristan's finger on his wedding-night, makes him think at once of the promise he had made to the queen, his true beloved (Sn.[1], ll.385 ff., compare especially Sn[1], ll.407-08 and T.[1], ll.39-40). Thomas is suggesting that any attempt on Tristan's part to find lasting consolation through another, be it a statue or a second

Iseut, is a mistake and bound to fail.

The new, invented episode is also made to serve a narrative purpose. At the end of T.[1] comes the *Eau hardie* incident, as a result of which Tristan's wife confesses to her brother, Kaherdin, that her marriage is still unconsummated. Kaherdin is naturally concerned for his sister and his anxiety is noticed by Tristan, who tells him of the beauty of the Queen Iseut and of her servant, Brengain. Eventually he brings Kaherdin to the underground chamber, where his brother-in-law is so dazzled by the statue of Brengain that he insists on being taken by Tristan to see the original (for these events see *1*, vol. I, pp.325-32). Thus, through the *Salle aux images* episode, a logical explanation is provided for their journey to England. Kaherdin, unlike Tristan, is not ready to seek satisfaction in an imitation of life.

When they reach England, they witness the *Cortège de la reine*, an incident which is *not* of Thomas's invention, but which he has certainly modified for his own particular purposes. Eilhart includes the scenes (*O*, ll.6264-6630) and probably at least the main lines of his story were also to be found in Thomas's source. In *O*, one reason for the journey is distinctly whimsical: Tristan must make good his boast to Kaherdin that 'there is a lady who for my sake, alone and in front of others, treats a dog better than your sister has treated me' (*12*, p.118). Thomas rejects this out of hand; Tristan and Kaherdin travel to England, one to see Iseut, the other to seek out the Brengain he has so far viewed only in likeness:

> E vunt s'ent dreit vers Engleterre
> Ysolt veeir e Brengien querre;
> Ker Kaerdin veeir la volt,
> E Tristran volt veeir Ysolt.
>
> (Str.[1], ll.1-4)

In its complete form, Thomas's episode may have had one or two odd features. For example, the dog which accompanies the queen, a traditional motif and essential to the story as told by Eilhart, has no real function in the remodelled episode. Even in the manuscript fragment that survives, one element at least may disconcert. Why does Kaherdin, espying the washerwomen and the chambermaids in the procession, believe he has identified Iseut and Brengain, when he has already gazed intently upon their almost living likenesses in the *Salle aux images*? But this is churlish criticism. An episode which in Thomas's source could have had dangerous consequences for Tristan (indeed, in *O*, Tristan informs Tînas that his life is in danger), has been transformed into a lighthearted, almost a comic passage, dependent for its effect upon the series of erroneous identifications made by the eager Kaherdin:

> Atant eis lur les lavenderes
> E les foraines chamberreres
> Ki servent del furain mester,
> Del liz aturner, del eshalcer,
> De dras custre, des chiés laver,
> Des altres choses aprester.
> Dunc dit Kaerdin: 'Or la vei.'
> — 'Ne vus, dit Tristran, par ma fei!'
>
> (Str.[1], ll.39-46)

There is certainly a sense of growing expectation, which presumably culminated in the appearance of Iseut and Brengain, distinguished by their extraordinary beauty from their merely beautiful precursors, but there is no tension in the scene.

Towards the beginning of the episode, Thomas declares his aim of keeping his story as short as possible:

> Que valt que l'um alonje cunte,
> U die ce que n'i amunte?
> Dirrai la sume et la fin.
>
> (Str.[1], ll.5-7)

Conventional though this formula may be, it is the one he has chosen to express rather than an opposite formula, such as 'que vus cuntereie plus?' Moreover, it is a formula which he puts into practice, not only in this episode but elsewhere in the text.

This is not to say that Thomas does not dwell on certain passages
when he considers it necessary. In the *Eau hardie* incident he
includes a section in which, as Dubois has explained (see *18*), the
movements of Iseut's horse and of Iseut herself are very
precisely detailed (T.[1], ll.206-22). But Thomas does not indulge
in gratuitous development of incident, and more typical of his
narrative manner is his very cursory account of Tristan's
wedding in Sn.[1], where he only really summons up sufficient
energy to tell us that the normal kind of thing happened:

> La messe dit li capeleins
> E quanque i affirt al servise,
> Solunc l'ordre de sainte eglise;
> Pois vont cum a feste mangier,
> Enaprés esbanier
> A quintaines, as cembels,
> As gavelocs e as rosels,
> As palastres, as eschermies,
> A gieus de plusurs aaties,
> Cum a itel feste affirent
> E cum cil del siecle requirent.
>
> (Sn.[1], ll.374-84)

He makes no attempt to name the participants in the games and
it later becomes obvious that he has not selected the activities he
lists with any great care. In the Douce fragment the queen starts
to wear a 'bruine' (probably a painful form of corselet) next to
her skin, in order to suffer as she believes her lover is suffering.
Learning of this, Tristan returns to England with Kaherdin.
Thomas's account is then astonishingly abrupt: the meeting of
the lovers at court is not described and can only be surmised (D.,
ll.792-94) and Thomas does not even bother to mention Iseut by
name. Things do not get any better as the episode progresses, for
Tristan then takes part in a sports competition and the games
played, so we discover, are the usual ones, very much the same
as were played at Tristan's wedding (compare especially Sn.[1],
l.381 and D., l.799). Then, a friend is suddenly introduced to
explain why Tristan and Kaherdin have horses:

> Tristan i fud reconeüz,
> D'un sun ami aparceüz:
> Dous chevals lur duna de pris,
> Nen aveit melliurs el païs.

(D., ll.809-12)

A similar conventional figure, though playing a different role, appears at roughly the same point in *O* (ll.7742-96), he probably appeared as well in the common source, and Thomas has not taken the trouble to invent a more original expedient. Admittedly, he does make the episode serve a purpose, for it rounds off the sequence that began with the quarrel of Iseut and Brengain: it was Cariado, Thomas's invented character, who provoked the quarrel with his false information and now, his usefulness exhausted, he is killed by Kaherdin in accordance with the promise made by Tristan to Brengain a little earlier (D., ll.712-16). Their mission accomplished, Tristan and Kaherdin hurry back to Brittany, thus bringing to an end the second and last of Tristan's secret visits. Eilhart has four returns to England, but Thomas is not the kind of writer who needlessly multiplies incident and he does not wish to include absolutely everything in his own version. 'Ne vol pas *trop* en uni dire' is what he tells us.

What is now emerging is that Thomas has limited interests in narrative as such. He is prepared to invent episodes, such as the *Verger* and *Salle aux images* episodes, if they help to further the logic of his account. Similarly, he is prepared to modify inherited material, as he does in the *Cortège de la reine* episode, if he feels that the behaviour of his characters requires more rational motivation, if he feels that *raisun* can be better served. But there is no sign of a desire to complicate episodes by the introduction of new incident and characters, no hint of a wish to repeat successful episodes and no indication that he is willing to indulge in description for its own sake. Indeed, he does appear to be casual almost to the point of negligence when he is forced to insert a narrative passage such as the account of Tristan's wedding. This passage does suggest that Thomas's interests reside elsewhere, for as soon as it is decently possible Thomas returns in Sn.[1] to the psychological analysis which makes up the vast bulk of this section; the ring given to Tristan by Iseut slips from his finger, our hero 'entre en un pensé novel' (Sn.[1], l.396) and this 'pensé novel', his new state of mind, is then exposed at almost inordinate length. The *Salle aux images* episode, although it provides credible motivation for the journey to England, leads in much the same way into an analysis of the emotional state not only of Tristan, but also of Mark, his queen and of the second Iseut. In fact, a psychological examination of the four main characters is undertaken *twice*! One passage, T.[1], ll.152-83, has the same content, disposed in the same order, as the preceding passage (T.[1], ll.75-151). Consider again the material Thomas introduces into the scenes leading up to the death of the lovers in D. The storm which strikes Iseut's ship does bring about an increase in tension, but the description of the storm itself is contained in a relatively short passage of some twenty-five lines; it provokes, however, a monologue from Iseut in which she presents her thoughts in a passage eighty lines in length. Tristan's fatal wound comes from a different source in *T*, but the basic motif, unlike much in the scene, was meekly carried over from an earlier version (see D., ll.856-57) and the actual wounding is very tersely described (D., ll.1046-48), before Thomas swiftly moves on and concentrates on the effects of the wound and particularly upon Tristan's emotional reactions. If we turn our attention to passages of psychological interest in the text, we shall be getting nearer to our author's central concerns.

3. Psychology

'Mais c'est l'analyste qui nous domine'
(O. Jodogne)

When telling of the events leading up to the deaths of the lovers, Thomas introduces a new character, Tristan le Nain. This figure may be related to the character Nampetenis who appears at approximately the same point in *O*, but he is essentially an invention of Thomas. His narrative function is clear: it is while helping Tristan le Nain in the worthy cause of regaining his lady that Tristan receives his fatal wound. This is not, however, the sole function of the new character, for he seems to serve also to cast light upon the psychology of the main hero. Tristan and Kaherdin are returning one day from hunting when they encounter a knight hitherto unknown to them. This knight asks to be directed to the castle of 'Tristran l'Amerus'. Tristan reveals he is the man he is seeking, and the knight then discloses his own identity and tells his story: his lady has been abducted and he is now requiring Tristan's help in order to win her back. Tristan prevaricates, prepared to put off this task until the following day, but the knight brooks no delay, refuses to believe the real Tristan would act otherwise than immediately in the circumstances he has described and seeks to take his leave. Tristan then decides to go with him at once.

The very name Thomas gives his new character surely invites us to see him as a reflection of the main hero. Moreover, in spite of the epithet accompanying his name, he is not a dwarf at all:

> Lungs ert e grant e ben pleners,
> Armez ert e beas chevalers.

(D., ll.915-16)

Does his 'Little John' type of nickname suggest he is meant to be a partial, a small-scale representation of Tristan himself? Just as we must look upon him as other than his name suggests, must we also regard him not as a character in his own right but as Tristan's *alter ego*? Certainly the situation Tristan le Nain describes has obvious affinities with the situation of the hero. Both their respective ladies are at the same time in the possession of others. Tristan le Nain tells of the abduction by Estult:

> Estult l'Orgillius Castel Fer
> L'en a fait a force mener.
> Il la tent en sun castel,
> Si en fait quanques li est bel.

(D., ll.943-46)

At this time, Queen Iseut is living with King Mark, who, exactly as Estult behaves with the lady, 'Fait son bon quant il en volt' (T.[1], l.153). In presenting his situation, the knight uses terms already associated with Tristan himself: he suffers 'dolur' (D., l.947), 'tristur' (D., l.948) and 'pesance' (D., l.949), he lacks 'confort' (D., l.951), 'deport' (D., l.952), 'joie' (D., l.953) and 'delit' (D., l.953). In the marriage fragment (Sn.[1]), Tristan had employed much the same vocabulary in his speeches of self-analysis. Further, Thomas employs rhymes in this passage which he has used previously when concerned with the main hero: for example, the rhyme of ll.949-50, 'anguisse: puisse', has appeared already and on more than one occasion (see Sn.[1], ll.183-84, 397-98, 483-84). The association created here between the two Tristans is soon to be reinforced in the plea Tristan makes to Kaherdin. Tristan offers to become Kaherdin's liege-man, the same offer the 'dwarf' makes to Tristan in this episode (D., ll.969, 1163).

And it is not only with the hero that this new character has affinities, for he seems to have an emotional kinship with Iseut as well. The rhyme words, and indeed the general sentiments, of ll.951-52 recall the feelings of Iseut when she is about to separate from Tristan in the *Verger* episode:

> N'en puis senz li aveir confort:
> Quant jo perdu ai mon deport.

(D., ll.951-52)

Ja n'avrai mais, amis, deport.
Quant j'ai perdu vostre confort.

(C., ll.45-46)

(At a later point in the story, Iseut will also employ the familiar rhyme, 'anguisse: puisse' (D., ll.1693-94).) Again, the expression employed by the knight in D., l.1007, 'La ren el mund que plus aim', is reminiscent of earlier lines and emotions attributed to Iseut: 'De la ren del mund que plus creit' (D., l.72), 'La ren qu'ele plus solt amer' (D., l.610). The phraseology may be conventional, but its very existence does impel the reader to relate Tristan le Nain to Iseut and strengthens an awareness that this secondary character has more than a purely narrative function, for he serves as well to shed light upon the psychology of the main characters.

He may, in fact, suggest even more. If the 'dwarf' reflects the emotional state of Tristan and also that of Iseut, there is an implied equivalence between the emotions of the hero and heroine. Certainly, in the text as a whole, the theme of emotional parity, of emotional interdependence, is one which is constantly reasserting itself when Thomas explores the psychology of his main figures.

The theme appears briefly in the *Verger* episode. The bulk of the scene is made up of a speech from Tristan, followed by a speech from Iseut in which the queen does little more than echo sentiments already voiced by the hero. Tristan has spoken of the pain of separation, 'Tel duel ai por la departie' (C., l.29) and Iseut does precisely the same: 'Tel paine ai de la desevranche' (C., l.43). She cannot conceive that she will ever be happy again—'Ja n'avrai mais, amis, deport' (C., l.45)—and Tristan had earlier stated 'Ja n'avrai hait jor de ma vie' (C., l.30). Tristan has asked that the queen should continue to love him, in spite of physical separation (C., ll.33-34), and Iseut assures him that this will be the case (C., ll.49-50). Thomas is obviously indicating that the lovers experience identical emotions, that they love each other with equal force, but one might legitimately argue that he does this in a mechanical and unexciting manner.

The idea of the lovers' emotional parity is explored in much greater subtlety in the marriage episode, the next fragment to survive. The strictly narrative element in this scene is kept to a minimum. Thomas reports that Tristan wins the hand of the second Iseut and gains parental approval, but a mere four lines are assigned to this (Sn.[1], ll.365-68): his account of the wedding ceremony, as we have seen, is almost equally perfunctory (Sn.[1], ll.369-84). There is a longer narrative section in the episode, presented as a kind of anxious meditation by Iseut upon the present whereabouts of Tristan:

> Ne set pas qu'il est en Bretaigne;
> Encore le quide ele en Espaigne,
> La ou il ocist le jaiant,
> Le nevod a l'Orguillos grant.
>
> (Sn.[1], ll.661-64)

But the dominant figures in the tale then told are not Tristan and this nephew, but King Arthur and Orguillos, and Thomas himself acknowledges the almost complete irrelevance of the tale: 'A la matire n'afirt mie' (Sn.[1], l.729). This is not to say that he displays no concern at all here for narrative: he refers back to the *Verger* episode, he anticipates the consequences of his hero's decision to marry Iseut and he invents the detail of Iseut's ring slipping from his finger. But it is on passages of psychological interest that Thomas has concentrated his energies.

When the episode opens, Tristan has met Iseut aux Blanches Mains, whose name and beauty have caused him to look upon her with growing affection. His interest in her has been encouraged, notably by Kaherdin, and he must now consider how to behave in the situation that has developed. Tristan's first monologue runs from l.5 to l.182. It is addressed to Queen Iseut, as if she were present and needed to be convinced of the correctness of the action Tristan will ultimately propose, but the speech soon reveals itself as an interior debate in which the hero seeks to convince *himself* that he is right to marry Iseut aux Blanches Mains. Arguments which seem to arise spontaneously have a pre-ordained conclusion, which Tristan must bring himself to express, after dispelling any residual doubts.

At the beginning of the monologue, beset by self-pity, Tristan contrasts his unhappiness with the state of 'deduit', 'joie' and 'delit' he ascribes to the queen. He then indicates his jealousy of King Mark whom he presents as enjoying the pleasures which once were his. He reaches a form of conclusion in ll.21-23, namely that Iseut has forgotten him:

> Ço qu'aveir ne puis claim je quite,
> Car jo sai bien qu'il se delite;
> Ublié m'ad pur suen delit.[3]

This conclusion does not arise naturally from whatever evidence is available to Tristan, but is for him a necessary one. From now on he almost entirely abandons the fiction that he is trying to persuade an absent Iseut and openly concentrates on justifying to himself the attitudes he had adopted. He produces a string of excuses to explain why his relationship with the queen should now be abandoned. He is under pressure from another lady (Sn.[1], ll.29-34); he does not name her, but he is indicating the direction in which his mind is working. He then dismisses as valueless his love for the queen, since he extracts no physical satisfaction from that relationship (Sn.[1], ll.35-42): again, he is obliquely putting forward an argument in favour of marrying the second Iseut. He goes on to contrast his own steadfastness with the queen's fickleness and reiterates in forceful terms the notion that the queen has forgotten him (Sn.[1], ll.43-48).

Tristan then seems to correct himself: mindful of their emotional interdependence, he states in ll.55-58 that had Iseut ceased to be faithful to him his heart would have told him, a view he asserts again in ll.79-80. But these are sentiments Tristan does not welcome at this time. He claims he *does* feel a sense of separation—'Jo sent bien la departie' (Sn.[1], 1.82)—and that Iseut no longer really loves him. When Tristan returns to the defence of the queen at 1.95, he produces arguments he can

[3] In l.22, *il* does seem to be an error for *el*, in view of the fact that Iseut must be the subject of l.23.

manipulate to his own benefit. He repeatedly suggests that the
queen may have forgotten him (see Sn.[1], ll.97, 104, 106, 118)
and, whereas in ll.67-68 he had claimed that the weight of shared
experience prevented him from loving someone else, he now
asserts (significantly, the same rhymes, 'desir: languir' are
employed) that if she finds satisfaction with Mark she has no
need to pine for another:

> Sa grant belté pas nel requirt,
> Ne sa nature n'i afirt,
> Quant de lui ad sun desir,
> Que pur altre deive languir.
>
> (Sn.[1], ll.99-102)

This means that he has no need to pine for her.

But soon Tristan feels the time has come to pay lip-service to
the opposite viewpoint. How can Iseut reject the past so lightly?
He counters this argument in ll.127-48 with a number of general
observations. He begins with a straightforward plea for
moderation, both in love and hate (Sn.[1], ll.135-36), but from
then on the train of thought is more tortuous. There seem to be
two interrelated ideas: the simpler is that one should love
goodness, 'franchise', and hate wickedness, 'co(i)lvertise' (Sn.[1],
ll.145-48); the second idea seems to be that if a person has
performed an act of 'franchise' and then an act of 'colvertise'
(as Tristan supposes Iseut to have done in turning to Mark), one
should remember the first act and not perform an act of
'colvertise' in return, for one act should almost cancel out the
other (Sn.[1], ll.137-42). He continues in ll.143-44 with an
imperative, urging, as in ll.135-36, the adoption of a moderate
line. The order of propositions is distinctly awkward here:
ll.145-48, which present the notions of 'franchise' and
'colvertise' in general terms, ought to precede the rest. But
presumably we are meant to see that Tristan is groping towards
self-persuasion rather than glibly producing a smooth set of
arguments.

Tristan now returns to his own particular situation,
comparing it as ever to that of Iseut. If the queen has loved him

in the past, he should not hate her now (Sn.[1], ll.149-52)[4], if she has forgotten her love for him, he can equally forget her and, since moderation is to be the policy, he should neither love her nor hate her. Thus, by assuming Iseut has forgotten him, he now feels justified in withdrawing from the relationship, exactly as he chooses to believe she has done. But this is not all. He develops the idea of what he sees as an identity of situation and now persuades himself that in marrying and seeking sexual pleasure with Iseut aux Blanches Mains he is really acting out of consideration for Queen Iseut. How can he really understand her situation if he himself does not marry? She has a husband, he must have a wife. In tones of magnanimity and almost of self-sacrifice, he finally openly declares his intention of marrying the second Iseut:

> Jo voil espuser la meschine
> Pur saveir l'estre a la reïne.
>
> (Sn.[1], ll.173-74)

Wilfully choosing to think the worst of Iseut, Tristan has deliberately perverted the laudable ideal of seeking emotional identity with his partner, in the interests of his own self-gratification.

Tristan's lapse turns out to be only temporary. On his wedding night, when he sees the ring which has slipped from his finger, Tristan experiences a sharp sense of remorse for what he has done and intended to do, remembers the promise of fidelity he made in the garden and now speaks out without a trace of self-deception: '*De parfunt cuer* jette un suspir' (Sn.[1], l.410). Whereas in the first monologue he sought to justify the demands of the body, in his second monologue he recognizes the primacy of the heart. He admits, in ll.421-23, that he never really considered Queen Iseut, in spite of all the noises he made about identifying with her position. He then presents his dilemma: should he betray the queen and break the promise he made her by consummating his marriage, or should he refuse to perform

---

[4] A comma, rather than Wind's full stop, should be printed after l.151, for l.152 should be associated with the preceding lines.

his conjugal duties?

> Senz grant pechié, senz mal faire
> Ne me puis d'iceste retraire,
> Ne jo n'i pois assembler
> Si jo ne mei voil desleer,
> Car tant ai vers Ysolt fait
> Que n'est raisun que ceste m'ait.
>
> (Sn.[1], ll.429-34)

This essential dilemma, once stated, is then reiterated in a series of different guises. There are one or two new ideas. Tristan can now bring himself to admit that revenge upon the queen was a motive behind his decision to marry (Sn.[1], ll.489-92); also, in ll.509-14, he anticipates that he would perform inadequately with his wife and she would realize he was in love with another. Indeed, it eventually happens that because of his *emotional* link with Queen Iseut he is *physically* unable to consummate his marriage (Sn.[1], ll.595-608): love triumphs over the senses. Tristan also moves towards a decision. He resolves to remain loyal to the queen, to enter his wife's bed, but to do no more, thus imposing upon himself a form of penance for once having doubted Iseut's fidelity: he will suffer if he feels desire for his wife; he will suffer if, without desire, he is forced to share her bed. By carrying out this painful penance, by resisting temptation, Tristan hopes the queen will forgive him:

> 'Pur ço qu'a Ysolt ment ma fei,
> Tel penitance preng sur mei,
> Quant ele savra cum sui destreit
> Par tant pardoner le mei deit.'
>
> (Sn.[1], ll.585-88)

When Queen Iseut finally appears in person in the episode, her faithfulness to her partner is made plain. Unlike Tristan, she has no designs on any one else:

> Ele nen ad altre voleir
> Ne altre amur, ne altre espeir,

En lui est trestuit sun desir.

(Sn.[1], ll.653-55)

We also learn something of her emotional state in the final, difficult passage in the episode, which tells of how she is approached by Cariado. This character is an invention of Thomas's but conforms to a stock type, the *beau couard*, the 'Handsome Coward'. Cariado believes that Tristan has now disappeared from Iseut's life and wants to take his place. He comes upon Iseut singing a sad love-song to herself, the 'lai de Guiron', and introduces his theme via a conceit, trying to act as the 'gabeeres' (Sn.[1], l.816), the wit, he is said to be:

> Trove Ysolt chantant un lai,
> Dit en riant: 'Dame, bien sai
> Que l'en ot fresaie chanter
> Contre de mort home parler,
> Car sun chant signefie mort;
> E vostre chant, cum jo record,
> Mort de fresaie signifie:
> Alcon ad ore perdu la vie.'

(Sn.[1], ll.817-24)

Cariado is perhaps suggesting that Iseut is singing of her own death, which the news of Tristan's marriage may well cause, but this seems unlikely, since his aim is surely to supplant Tristan in her affections, rather than to produce her departure from the world.Although to imply any association at all is far from flattering, Cariado does seem to intend a contrast between the song of Iseut and the song of the 'fresaie', a breed of owl, commonly a bird of ill-omen.[5]. Whereas the owl sings of the death of a man, Iseut must be singing of the death of a 'fresaie' (see *45*, p.43): just as Guiron in the song is lost to the lady, so Tristan, Cariado is hoping to go on to explain, is dead, in that he is now lost to Iseut through his marriage. In an angry but

---

[5] See, for example, *Piramus et Tisbé*, ed. by C. de Boer (Paris, Champion, 1921), ll.635-39: 'Toner oï de desus destre,/Senti tot le palais fremir/Et vit la lune empalir,/Vit le huant, vit la fresaie,/Mais nis uns signes ne l'esmaie'.

controlled reaction, Iseut continues the conceit. If Cariado chooses to interpret her song as he does, he must be the 'fresaie' who should fear for his life, for, like the 'fresaie', he is a bearer of bad news. Cariado, taken aback, retaliates boorishly. If the queen predicts his death, she must be the 'fresaie', while he accepts the allied term, 'huan', which she wished upon him in 1.827. Wishing only to harm Iseut now, he tells her she has lost Tristan: the 'fresaie' he had in mind to start with is dead as far as she is concerned. Cariado crudely tells her that she will have to look around for someone else now that Tristan has married amidst great splendour, 'a grant honor' (Sn.[1], 1.862).[6] The queen refuses to stoop to the level of Cariado, accepts the role of 'fresaie' and says her bad news for him is that she rejects him out of hand:

> 'Ne vos ne vostre droerie
> N'amerai ja jor de m[a vie.]
> Malement porcha[cé me oüsse,]
> Se vostre amor re[ceüse.]
> Milz voil la sue aveir perdue
> Que vostre amor receüe,
> Tele novele dit m'avez
> Dunt ja certes pro nen avrez.'
>
> (Sn.[1], ll.873-80)[7]

Left alone again, Iseut cannot help but feel distress, anger and the same 'dolor' as was experienced by the lady in her song at the loss of Guiron. Her loyalty to Tristan, so it would seem, has brought her scant reward. But at this point the fragment ends: only in the first sections of the Douce manuscript will there come a full account of Iseut's reaction to what she has just heard.

The main substance of the first part of D, is a quarrel between Brengain and Iseut, which, so the derivative versions suggest,

---

[6] Or is 'a grant honor' to be associated with 'femme'? Is Cariado suggesting that Tristan has taken a wife belonging to the landed gentry, hence the reference to her family in 1.863? Or is he insinuating that whereas Tristan's wife is a lady of great honour, the queen is nothing of the kind?

[7] The passage has been repunctuated at ll.874 and 875, where the lines as presented by Wind make little sense.

was less than perfectly prepared. After the *Cortège de la reine* events, Tristan and Kaherdin have remained in England. Brengain allows Kaherdin to sleep in her bed, but for two nights she deceives him with the aid of a magic cushion, which, placed beneath his head, immediately sends him into a deep sleep. On the third night, however, at the instigation of Iseut, Brengain discards the cushion and responds enthusiastically to Kaherdin's advances. The magic cushion appears also in *O* and was, therefore, probably also in the source Eilhart shared with Thomas. The precise nature of the incident in the common source necessarily remains unknown, but Eilhart may well have undertaken a fairly radical transformation of his material at this point (ll.6672-6804): it is, for example, a relatively new character, Gymele, who plays the role attributed to Brengain in *T*. In fact, the cushion makes little sense in the hands of Brengain, for, if its purpose was to protect a maiden's virginity, *her* virginity has long since been lost. In the French version, the cushion is reduced to little more than a comic device which Thomas might very easily have abandoned altogether. But whatever form the original story took, by continuing with Brengain, Thomas achieves a concentration of character which is lacking in *O*. This same concentration of character is seen in the precise incident which occasions Brengain's outburst against Iseut. In *O*, a new figure, Pleherin, is introduced (ll.6828-31), but Thomas re-employs Cariado. It is Cariado who claims to have put Tristan and Kaherdin to flight, when it was only their squires he had been pursuing: he informs Brengain that she has given herself to a coward and then she angrily accuses the queen of engineering her apparent dishonour. Not one to multiply incidents unnecessarily, Thomas does not multiply character either.

It is once again becoming clear that it is upon psychological aspects that Thomas concentrates his attention. Here he exposes at length the feelings of Brengain and Iseut, who are caught up in an intense quarrel of the kind only possible between characters whose previous lives have been intimately associated. For Brengain, Iseut's act of treachery in persuading her to give herself to an unworthy knight has proved to be the last straw.

She details what she has done for the queen and Tristan. She lost her virginity to protect Iseut, but the only reward she received was that her murder was arranged. She forgave—foolishly, she thinks—this crime committed against her, but this time, after Iseut has caused her shame as a result of yielding to the cowardly Kaherdin, she is intent on revenge:

> 'Ço fud par vostre entisement.
> Jon averai ben le vengement
> De vus, de Tristran vostre ami:
> Ysolt, e vus e lui deffi;
> Mal en querrai e damage
> Pur la vilté de ma huntage.'
>
> (D., ll.64-69)

This section of the Douce fragment casts light not only on Brengain but inevitably also on Iseut and Tristan, the objects of her resentment (when recapitulating in ll.477-91, Thomas is careful to point out that all the characters, Mark and Cariado included, interrelate emotionally). In spite of immediate appearances, Iseut exhibits no disloyalty towards Tristan. For her first response to Brengain's outburst, she adopts a conciliatory approach, affecting self-pity:

> Suspire et dit: 'Lasse, caitive!
> Grant dolz est que jo tant sui vive,
> Car unques nen oi se mal nun
> En ceste estrange regiun.'
>
> (D., ll.82-85)

She then flatters her companion by naming what she, the queen, has lost through Tristan (D., ll.86 ff.), exactly as Brengain had indicated what she had lost as a result of her association with the lovers. Iseut further flatters her by referring to her past loyalty (D., l.108) and even goes so far as to curse Tristan ('A qui Deus en duinst grant contraire!' (D., l.131)), much as Brengain had done at the beginning of her speech ('Ki Deu doinst ui mal aventure' (D., l.11). This approach fails in the end. When Brengain seems resolved to tell Mark of her treachery, Iseut's exasperation with her breaks through: more than a little unfairly, she blames her for the way she and Tristan have behaved (D., ll.305-27) and claims that if any revenge is exacted Brengain is going to suffer as well (D., ll.328-36). But none of Iseut's genuine anger is directed against Tristan. In *O* and very probably in the common source, Iseut was angry with Tristan, but Thomas has modified his received data by making Brengain angry with the lovers and has allowed only a pale shadow of the original idea to remain, in Iseut's *feigned* anger with Tristan.

Iseut's true feelings for Tristan emerge later in the fragment, for her loyalty to her partner is made clear. Disguised as a leper, Tristan returns in order to see Iseut, but is maltreated at Brengain's instigation and the queen does not dare to intervene; he then goes into hiding, in despair because he thinks he has been rejected. He is discovered when close to death, goes on to persuade Brengain that she has been misinformed as to the identity of those who had fled from Cariado and is re-united with the queen. After Tristan returns to Brittany, Iseut starts to wear a 'bruine', the garb of the ascetic:

> E cele, qui est veire amie
> De pensers e de granz suspirs,
> E leise mult de ses desirs,
> Plus leale ne fud unc veüe,
> Vest une bruine a sa char nue.

> (D., ll.756-60)

In *O*, Iseut puts on a hair shirt before she achieves any form of reconciliation with Tristan, conscious that she was wrong to have believed him capable of cowardly flight (ll.7168-75). In *T*, however, her loyalty has never been in doubt; she puts on the garment in order to suffer as Tristan has suffered, in order to share the same emotional experiences:

> Pur les granz mals qu'il ad suffert
> Qu'a privé li ad descovert,

> Pur la peine, pur la dolur
> Que tant ad eü pur s'amur,
> Pur l'anguise, pur la grevance,
> Partir volt a la penitence.
>
> (D., ll.741-46)

The theme of emotional parity, touched on in the *Verger* episode, fully explored in the marriage scenes, reasserts itself once more. Iseut's 'penitance' is an attempt, so it would seem, to match Tristan's 'penitance' when he decided to lie with his wife and yet not consummate their marriage (see Sn.[1], ll.585-88). Perhaps it might be well to point out that, in spite of the religious terminology employed—Iseut's 'penitance', her mortification of the flesh through the 'bruine', the accompanying vow (D., ll.764-66), the journey of Tristan and Kaherdin disguised 'en penant' (D., l.789)—there is evidently no flight from the physical on the part of the lovers. In the concluding lines of the episode (D., ll.792-94), Tristan and Kaherdin reach court and the worldly nature of their activities there cannot really be much in doubt.

Tristan has really little to do in the episode except react to the treatment meted out to him by Iseut, the nature of which is controlled by Brengain. But when he does act of his own accord, he exhibits the same concern for the queen as Iseut so plainly shows for him. When Tristan decides to disguise himself and return to court, he does so in order to find out about Iseut:

> Tristan se prent a purpenser
> Que il s'en vait vileinement,
> Quant ne set ne quar ne coment
> A la reïne Ysolt estait.
>
> (D., ll.492-95)

Iseut reveals the same kind of anxiety for her partner before she puts on the 'bruine': 'Ne set pur veir cum li estait' (D., l.740). After Tristan is apparently rejected by Iseut, there is a description of his emotions, closely followed by a presentation of her very similar emotional state. Tristan weeps (D., l.588) and wonders why he remains alive (D., ll.600, 605), and Iseut, in turn, has much the same feelings, crying (D., l.612) and considering the world without attraction (D., ll.613-14). One senses that Thomas, through Brengain, has engineered a situation in which he can concentrate on the lovers' states of mind and, in particular, on the emotional distress they are both experiencing.

In the final section of Thomas's romance, there is a brief digression, an excursus, on *ire* (D., ll.1323-35). The passage arises naturally out of the circumstances of the scene, for anger is the dominant emotion immediately attributed to Tristan's wife ('El quer en ad mult grant irrur' (D., l.1340)), but it does interrupt the narrative flow and introduces observations of general import. Indeed, so harsh is Thomas's criticism of female extremism that his attempt at recantation in ll.1334-35 rings (deliberately?) very hollow: he has certainly *not* fought shy of saying exactly what he wants to say on this general subject. In the marriage episode, there is a much longer excursus on *novelerie* (Sn.[1], ll.233-304), on the desire for change and novelty and on human inconstancy, perhaps inspired by the *Disciplina clericalis* of Petrus Alfonsus (see *26* and especially *31*, pp.387-92). There is certainly in the passage an implied comment on Tristan's behaviour in particular: the abstract terms already used by Tristan, 'poeir', 'voleir', 'desir' and 'raisun', are re-introduced, as is the contrast between 'colvertise' and 'franchise'. But the passage does have a universal application — 'Cum *genz* sunt d'estrange nature' (Sn.[1], l.234) — and does seem to be inviting us to look beyond the narrow confines of the hero's individual psychology. In much the same way, Thomas is concerned with the nature of the love existing between Tristan and Iseut, but he is suggesting at the same time through them the nature of love in general and, moreover, how 'ideal' love, 'fine amur' (D., l.1679), can be identified. At the end of her angry exchanges with Iseut, Brengain goes at once to see Mark, apparently resolved to reveal everything she knows to the king:

> En cest curez e en ceste ire,
> Vait Brengain sun buen al rei dire.

> (D., ll.345-46)

But in the end she does nothing of the kind: she does not betray
Iseut, she merely suggests that the queen may misbehave in
future and, in a surprising twist Thomas gives to the narrative,
denounces not Tristan but Cariado. This is obviously one way of
taking revenge on Cariado, the man who taunted her with the
charge that her lover was a coward. But does Brengain's
behaviour indicate also, as Alison Adams suggests (*13*, p.89),
that she recognizes the superior nature of the lovers'
relationship? The exemplary form of Tristan's love in particular
emerges in the Tristan le Nain episode. The 'dwarf' has expressly
sought out the hero, since he is 'icil qui plus ad amé/De trestuz
ceus qui unt esté' (D., ll.963-64). Faced with the hero's delaying
tactics, the 'dwarf' claims that the real Tristan would
immediately have shown sympathy for his plight:

> Qui que vus seiét, baus amis,
> Unques ne amastes, ço m'est avis.
> Se seüsez que fud amisté,
> De ma dolur eussez pité.

(D., ll.987-90)

When Tristan shows pity and agrees to ride out at once (D.,
ll.1010-16), he is indicating that he does know what love is and
that he shares the view of Tristan le Nain as to its true nature.

Tristan le Nain is killed and Tristan himself is wounded in the
fight against Estult and his brothers. Kaherdin promises to take
a message to Iseut and then, in the long speech beginning at
l.1183, Tristan indicates to his friend what he should tell the
queen. In this speech are to be seen many of the essential
features of the lovers' relationship and also of love in general, as
Thomas understands it. It would seem, first of all, that there was
a kind of love existing between Tristan and Iseut before they
drank the potion:

> Dites li qu'ore li suvenge
> Des emveisures, des deduiz

Qu'eümes jadis jors e nuiz,
Des granz peines, des tristurs
E des joies e des dusurs
De nostre amur fine e veraie
Quant ele jadis guari ma plaie,
Del beivre qu'ensemble beümes
En la mer quant suppris en fumes.

(D., ll.1214-22)

One realizes the difficulties of interpreting from the evidence here (especially since the episode to which allusion is made is lost), but it does seem that an 'amur fine e veraie' existed when Tristan was looked after by Iseut when he first came to Ireland and was recovering from the wounds inflicted by the Morholt. Thomas suggests elsewhere, through the relationship of Brengain and Kaherdin, that love must first be a matter of personal choice, of personal commitment. Brengain enters fully into her liaison not blindly, not simply at her mistress's bidding, but knowingly, because she was convinced of Kaherdin's suitability, of his general worth. She uses the description ironically in her quarrel with Iseut, but when she gave herself to Kaherdin she was sure that 'Unc ne fud hum de sun barnage,/De sun pris, de sun vasselage' (D., ll.44-45). What is not clear, though, is whether the early attraction Tristan and Iseut felt for each other then developed into the emotional experience described in the poem or was destroyed and replaced by something rather different: the drinking of the potion may have crystallized the lovers' initial relationship, but it may equally well have vitiated it.

A prominent feature of the love emerges from this same passage. Tristan may begin by mentioning to Kaherdin the 'emveisures' and the 'deduiz' of love, but he is soon referring to the 'granz peines' and the 'tristurs' he has endured with Iseut. It may be dangerous to draw conclusions from only part of the romance, particularly when the tragic ending imposes a sombre colouring on the material. Nevertheless, in the extant fragments, the only real evidence we have, love and sorrow are frequently linked. At the beginning of the *Salle aux images* episode, Tristan

is said to recall as well as 'les deliz des granz amors', the
'travaus', 'dolors', 'paignes' and 'ahans' he has endured with
Iseut (T.[1], ll.1-4). In the scene in which the queen puts on the
'bruine', emphasis is placed upon what Tristan suffers as a
consequence of his love for her and what she, deliberately,
chooses to suffer in return:

> Mult suffre dure penitance
> Pur s'amur en mainte fesance,
> E mainte peine e maint ahan
> Suffre ceste Ysolt pur Tristran,
> Mesaise, dehait e dolur.
>
> (D., ll.767-71)

The Tristan le Nain episode goes so far as to suggest that, in
Thomas's view, grief is the sign of love, the emotion that
guarantees its authenticity. Because Tristan fails to react
appropriately to his distress, the 'dwarf' cannot believe he is
really Tristan l'Amerus:

> Jo sai que, si Tristran fuissét,
> La dolur qu'ai sentissét,
> Car Tristran si ad amé tant
> Qu'il set bien que mal unt amant.
>
> (D., ll.979-82)

Happiness, when it occurs, is only fleetingly reported: when
Tristan and Iseut are re-united after Brengain is persuaded she
was mistaken, virtually all Thomas says is that 'Tristran a Ysolt
se deduit' (D., l.723).

Inevitably, love causes pain to innocent parties. After his
reunion with the queen, Tristan returns to Brittany and to his
wife, who, realizing he loves another, can only grieve:

> Ben li est enditee l'amur,
> El quer en ad mult grant dolur
> E grant pesance e deshait,
> Tut son eür li est destrait.

> Coment il aime l'altre Ysolt,
> Ço est l'achaisun dunt ore s'en dolt.
>
> (D., ll.731-36)

In fact, when Thomas intervenes in the text and introduces his analysis of the emotional states of his four main characters, he points out that 'dolur' is experienced by *all* the parties concerned, by Tristan and his wife, by Iseut and her husband:

> Entre ces quatre ot estrange amor:
> Tut en ourent painne e dolur,
> E un e autre en tristur vit;
> E nuls d'aus nen i a deduit.
>
> (T.[1], ll.71-74)

On occasion there is the hint that love might be associated with pleasure. There is such a suggestion when Tristan reveals his intention not to consummate his marriage to the second Iseut. 'Amur', the kind of love to which Tristan decides to adhere, contrasts with 'delit', mere carnal satisfaction:

> Encuntre amur achaison quer,
> Pur mei en ceste delitier.
> Ne dei trichier pur mun delit
> Tant cum Ysolt m'amie vit.
>
> (Sn.[1], ll.561-64)

But 'amur' includes sexual love, referred to as 'desir' in l.538:

> Ore me harra par l'astenir
> Pur ço qu'el n'at sun desir,
> Car ço est que plus alie
> En amor amant e amie.
>
> (Sn.[1], ll.537-40)

Yet 'amur' is more than sexual love: indeed, it embraces a moral force which effectively prevents sexual fulfilment with any one other than his beloved (see Sn.[1], ll.509-14, 597-600). However, rather than the possible pleasures, it is the pains generated by love which dominate. After pointing out that where 'dolor' relates to the suffering endured by Tristan and Iseut it rhymes twenty-eight times with 'amor', Phyllis Johnson goes on to make the pertinent comment that 'le lecteur, l'auditoire plutôt, bercé par une telle fréquence, associe bientôt le thème de la douleur à celui de l'amour' (see *30*, p.548).

But whatever sorrows their relationship may bring, lovers must remain loyal to each other. Tristan tells Kaherdin to inform Iseut of his continuing fidelity (D., ll.1249-54). Elsewhere, Tristan asks himself why he married 'Contre l'amur, cuntre la fei/Qu'a Ysolt m'amie dei?' (Sn.[1], ll.553-54), while it is as a mark of her attachment to Tristan that Iseut — 'Plus leale ne fud unc veüe' (D., l.759) — puts on her 'bruine'. This loyalty must not give way to social or religious pressures: Tristan knows what the consequences of failing to consummate his marriage will be (see Sn.[1], ll. 500-02), but in the end he holds firm. Moreover, loyalty knows no limits. Faced with the prospect of losing his lady forever, Tristan le Nain can see no other outcome but his own death:

> E! Deus, pur quei ne pus murir
> Quant perdu ai que plus desir?
>
> (D., ll.1001-02)

Certainly the love of Tristan and Iseut is closely associated with death in the final episodes of the romance. Tristan tells Kaherdin of the potion drunk at sea, and then he adds:

> El beivre fud la nostre mort,
> Nus n'en avrum ja mais confort;
> A tel ure duné nus fu
> A nostre mort l'avum beü.
>
> (D., ll.1223-26)

Tristan asserts here that it is not his poisoned wound, but the love he shares with Iseut, represented by the philtre, which will cause his death. Hearing of the black sail and believing himself abandoned by Iseut, he will die at once; Iseut similarly, finding her lover dead, will succumb immediately. Neither can live without the other. Much the same idea is expressed by Gottfried in the French refrain he includes, which may easily have come from Thomas's text:

> 'Isot ma drue, Isot mamie,
> En vus ma mort, en vus ma vie!'
>
> (ll. 19409-10)

Again, in the *Salle aux images* episode, Tristan grieves for the absent Iseut, 'La bele raïne, sa amie,/En cui est sa mort e sa vie' (T.[1], ll. 121-22). But one can perhaps say more. When Tristan and Iseut drink the potion and the kind of love which they will share is either established or confirmed, they are not free agents, for at that time, 'A tel ure', Iseut is on her way to Cornwall and to her marriage with Mark. Is Thomas indicating that because the love had become *socially* impossible, it must inevitably bring an absence of *confort* and end in death?

4. *Style*

'Ce précieux, ce maître du syl-
logisme sentimental' (J. Larmat)

Queen Iseut's journey to Brittany, her mission of mercy to the
dying Tristan, is delayed first by a storm, then by a calm, but
eventually a favourable wind brings her to shore. There, she
hears bells ringing and the sound of lamentation in the streets.
Somebody has to tell her that all this is happening because of the
death of her lover and, to fulfil this narrative purpose, Thomas
invents the character of an old man, an 'anciens' (D., 1.1787).
But Thomas does more than is really necessary, for he produces
a carefully worked out and balanced speech. After the
introductory line, 1788, the old man first indicates the great
extent of their loss (D., ll.1789-90), sentiments he reiterates at
the close (D., ll.1797-98). A statement to the effect that Tristan
is dead then follows (D., 1.1791), to be paralleled later by
ll.1795-96. The central part of the passage, ll.1792-94, describes
the concern Tristan showed for others. In fact, Thomas has
deliberately chosen to introduce here features typical of the
planctus, the lament at the death of the hero, and the presence of
this *planctus* in the text is an indication that Thomas is very
much aware of the characteristic literary procedures of his day.
Further, as Valeria Bertolucci Pizzorusso (see *15*) and F.M.
Warren (see *47*) have shown, Thomas is fully acquainted with
the rhetorical devices commonly employed to ornament texts of
his period. Bertolucci Pizzorusso, in particular, is adept at
identifying the devices our author uses, but perhaps fails to
gauge properly their purpose or their appropriateness to the
context. Rather than simply stick a label on a stylistic feature,
we need to recognize its function and assess its effectiveness.

If Thomas was a 'clerc', as previously surmised, he will have
acquired his knowledge of literary composition as he progressed

through the schools. In the medieval curriculum, grammar, rhetoric and dialectic, the arts of communication, formed the *trivium*, the first set of subjects to be studied. Sometimes poetry came under the wing of grammar, sometimes under the wing of rhetoric, branches of the *trivium* concerned with the reading of the major authors of antiquity. Pupils were by no means passive recipients of knowledge, for they were required to compose, to imitate the manner and technique of the authors they studied. To aid them in their labours and to give general instruction in the use of verse, their masters produced technical manuals, which were essentially treatises on rhetoric as applied to poetry: the art of speaking attractively came to the aid of the art of writing attractively. These treatises may not offer very exciting reading, but they do represent what Thomas and other would-be writers were taught about the poetic craft. As Faral has pointed out, these works were not 'des élucubrations stériles; les écrivains s'en sont nourris' (*19*, p.xvi).

Of these manuals, the *Poetria Nova* of Geoffrey of Vinsauf (see *19*, pp.194-262), a work of just over two thousand Latin hexameters, enjoyed considerable vogue. First of all, Geoffrey considers the various ways of beginning and ending a poem (*dispositio*), and then moves on to the means whereby a text can be expanded (*amplificatio*). He identifies eight methods, including *interpretatio*, the art of presenting the same idea in different ways, and *apostrophatio* or *exclamatio*, the appeal directed at some animate or inanimate object; he also inserts two passages which illustrate the working of description (*descriptio*). Geoffrey says a little about the opposite process, how to treat a theme with brevity (*abbreviatio*), before devoting himself in the longest section of his work to stylistic ornament. He distinguishes between 'difficult' and 'easy' ornaments. The 'difficult' ornaments are the ten tropes, a trope being a device in which a word is employed in a sense other than its normal one. Under this heading come metaphor (*translatio*) and metonymy (*denominatio*). The 'easy' ornaments, far more numerous, are the figures, where words maintain their everyday senses and effects are produced from clever and unusual patterns of words and thoughts. The figures are then divided between figures of speech and figures of thought. Whatever individual qualities medieval theorists may have, they all share a mania for classification. Amongst the figures of speech Geoffrey includes examples of *annominatio*, word play of various kinds, and of chiasmus (*commutatio*), where the order of words in the first of a pair of balanced clauses is reversed in the second. The figures of thought are on the whole less important, but inserted at this point in the treatise is *frequentatio*, a popular method of amplification involving the accumulation of arguments and facts (see *33*, pp.241-42). Geoffrey ends his work with a number of general observations, some more pertinent than others.

The *Poetria Nova* was probably written between 1208 and 1213, some time after Thomas finished his work. But, since all the treatises on poetry written in the twelfth century and up to the middle of the thirteenth century contain similar teaching, there is little reason to doubt that Thomas received the same kind of instruction that Geoffrey dispenses. Naturally, there are many occasions in his romance when Thomas does not choose to exercise his acquired skills to the full, particularly if his interest is not completely engaged. The *Cortège de la reine* episode contained in the Strasbourg fragment is essentially light-hearted in tone, so Thomas obviously has no wish to over-load it with too many complicated varieties of ornamentation. True, he does introduce a form of *frequentatio*:

> Vienent garzun, vienent varlet,
> Vienent seuz, vienent brachet
> E li curliu e li veltrier
> E li cuistruns e li bernier
> E marechals e herberjurs.
>
> (Str.[1], ll.25-29)

This stringing-together of pairs of near-synonyms is a fairly simple technique, one which almost implies negligence rather than attention on our author's part. A little later in the text, at l.44, Thomas definitely allows the list of the chambermaids' duties to tail off very weakly, which suggests that he is not really exerting himself at this point. There are attempts at introducing balanced passages: at l.50, there is a four-line section beginning 'Apres', describing the males in the party, followed, at l.55, by another four-line section, similarly begun by 'Apres', in which the females are described. This is not an unattractive procedure, but again Thomas does not seem to be really making an effort. He has obviously not bothered to vary his vocabulary much either: his casual approach has already allowed him to write 'foraines' in l.40 and 'furain' in l.42 (we also find 'fureines' in l.47), and now 'bels' crops up in both l.52 and l.53, while 'ensegnéz' (l.52) will soon be followed by 'enseignéz' in l.59.

I have been dealing here with a largely narrative passage and, as I have suggested in a previous chapter, Thomas's interest in narrative as such is strictly limited and a relatively relaxed piece of writing is to be expected. Moreover, Thomas is unlikely to devote his fullest attention to an episode where a relatively minor character such as Kaherdin generally holds the centre of the stage. Other narrative passages show similar stylistic features to those exhibited here. In the brief account of the marriage ceremony (Sn.[1], ll.369-84), we find the use of *frequentatio* in ll.379-82 — which speeds up the rhythm of the passage and suggests Thomas's eagerness to get to the end of it — and the same kind of limp finish in ll.383-84 that we found at l.44 of the *Cortège* scene and which similarly suggests Thomas's desire to move on to other things. In the Douce fragment, the account of the conflict between the two Tristans and the family of Estult is very short, unornamented and shows signs of sloppy writing. Estult's brothers are 'hardiz' and 'pruz' in l.1027 and these same terms are applied, only a few lines later, at l.1042, to the two Tristans; how many brothers are killed in each of the various encounters is not immediately clear and to whom or to what 'sun' refers in l.1036 is a matter of some debate. (Does 'sun apel' mean 'the call made upon him', upon 'li sires'?) Thomas does not even go out of his way to invent original names for his characters, for 'Estult l'Orgillus Castel Fer' recalls 'l'Orguillos grant'. It is true that Thomas devotes greater care to one particular passage of narrative, his account of the storm which delays Iseut's ship (D., ll.1587-1614). The storm is skilfully introduced, the main clause with its announcement of the wind getting up deliberately being held back until l.1592. Line 1591 must be a parenthetical statement (and should be punctuated accordingly) and the presence of this parenthesis makes the wind even more unexpected. For the bulk of his account, Thomas may then have drawn on Wace's description of storms at sea and other conventional descriptions elsewhere, but, as Joël Grisward has pointed out (see *24*), he has succeeded in combining familiar elements in a precise, logical and poetic manner.

Nevertheless, Thomas characteristically concentrates his attention not on external, physical phenomena but on the storm within, on the mental torment Iseut is experiencing at this point in the story. The queen, if not quite devoid of hope, rarely envisages a happy outcome to her trials. Indeed, she seems to have long anticipated a joint death with Tristan:

> Amis, jo fail a mun desir,
> Car en voz bras quidai murrir.
>
> (D., ll.1649-50)

As Lefay-Toury has pointed out (see *35*, p.182), Iseut regularly presents death in these lines as if it were the only possible conclusion to her relationship with Tristan. To support this important notion, Thomas has given his heroine a long, elaborate monologue (D., ll.1615-94), which is held together by a number of recurrent features. In the course of the monologue, the queen frequently mentions God's will and her acceptance of His ruling: 'Deus ne volt pas' (l.1616), 'Se Deus volsist' (l.1627), 'Quant Deu la volt' (l.1636), 'se Deu le vult' (l.1664) (see also ll.1675 and 1692). The passage is further punctuated by regular calls upon Tristan, after the initial apostrophizing of the absent, dying hero in l.1619: 'Tristran' (ll.1668, 1684), 'beals amis' (l.1621), 'bels amis' (l.1658), 'amis' (ll.1633, 1637, 1649, 1665, 1672, 1680, 1685, 1693). There are frequent exclamations (ll.1615, 1664, 1692-94) and rhetorical questions (ll.1665, 1680-84). Iseut's speech is rich in hypotheses (ll.1619-20, 1627-28, 1688-89) and the certainties she brings forth in the first part of her speech — 'Ben sai' (l.1622), 'Jo sai ben' (l.1638), 'E ben sai' (l.1648) — are balanced by the doubts introduced into the second part (*dubitatio* or *correctio*) — 'Ne sai' (l.1666), 'Ne sai' (l.1672), 'Ne sai' (l.1687), 'ne sai' (l.1690). One might also mention the way in which pronouns of the first and second persons are made to form a chiasmus, as at ll.1688-89 (cf. also ll.1641-42):

> Mais, se mort fussez devant mei,
> Apruef vus curt terme vivreie.

There, in ll.1639-48, Iseut presents an elaborate series of syllogisms, apparently to convince herself that she will not die alone:

> De tel manere est nostre amur
> Ne puis senz vus sentir dolur;
> Vus ne poez senz moi murrir,
> Ne jo senz vus ne puis perir.
> Se jo dei em mer periller,
> Dun vus estuet a tere neier:
> Neier ne poez pas a tere;
> Venu m'estes en la mer querre.
> La vostre mort vei devant mei,
> E ben sai que tost murrir dei.

Another recurrent feature one might identify is the rhyme 'confort: mort' (and 'mort: confort'), which appears four times, at ll.1621-22, 1633-34, 1669-70 and 1683-84. No other set of rhyme-words appears more than once and, like other recurrent features listed already, the repetition of these rhyme-words helps to hold the passage together. One might also say that the repeated rhyme-words lend the monologue its particular flavour, serving as a kind of mnemonic to remind us of a basic theme, namely the inconsolability and helplessness which will be experienced by one partner on hearing of the death of the other. The device seems a deliberate one, for Thomas has chosen to employ it elsewhere. The only set of rhyme-words which appears more than once in the two long speeches by Tristan le Nain is 'amur: dolur' (D., ll.983-84, 991-92), and once again these rhyme-words suggest a major theme of the episode, the association between love and suffering on which the 'dwarf' insists. The same device is employed a little later, not in a monologue this time but in the section which explains why Tristan's wife acts as she does, ll.1323-66 of the Douce fragment. The passage is carefully framed, beginning as it does with a general observation, 'Ire de femme est a duter' (D., l.1323), and concluding with the comment that Iseut's behaviour is inspired by her anger: 'Car ire a ço la comuet' (D., l.1366). Not surprisingly, this idea is continued by the only set of rhyme-words to be repeated in the scene, 'amur: irrur' (D., ll.1339-40, 1357-58). We are forcibly reminded that Hell has no 'Fury like a Woman scorn'd'.

But is all the care exercised by Thomas in writing Iseut's monologue really worthwhile? With characteristic verve, Pauphilet has condemned the whole speech (see *40*, p.137), and one must admit that Thomas does not display a consistent sureness of touch. Iseut's observation in l.1645, to the effect that Tristan will find it impossible to drown on land, while it does lead in the next line to the important notion of the lovers' being united at sea, is nothing if not self-evident. The idea of emotional interdependence, central to the psychology of the main characters, is then pursued and could be viewed as being carried to absurd lengths, when Iseut puts forward the bizarre hope that, if she and Tristan both drown, they could share a common grave in the belly of some great fish!

> Car, se jo dei neier ici,
> E vus, ço crei, devez neier,
> Uns peissuns poüst nus dous mangier;
> Eissi avrum par aventure,
> Bels amis, une sepulture.
>
> (D., ll.1654-58)

Elsewhere, Thomas's touch is more certain. The first section of the Douce fragment (ll.1-334) is, as we have seen, devoted to the quarrel between Iseut and her maid which has arisen because Brengain wrongly believes the queen has persuaded her to give herself to a coward. The section contains some familiar features. It is dominated by long speeches, one of which at least begins in a conventional manner (compare ll.82-83, the start of Iseut's reaction to Brengain's charges, with ll.1615-16). We find once again that a number of sets of rhyme-words are repeated: in her first speech, Brengain stresses that for her love has not brought honour ('amur: honur' (D., ll.8-9), 'honur: amur' (D., ll.32-33)), and in her third speech she stresses the dishonour presently accruing to Mark ('amur: desonur' (D., ll.287-88, 297-98)). But Brengain's speeches, as befits dialogue, do have a degree of naturalness which was missing from the monologue of Iseut analysed earlier. There are some stock rhetorical devices: we find *anaphora*, the repetition of the same words at the beginning of several successive clauses, in ll.37-40, *interpretatio* in ll.243-46 and *annominatio* in ll.271-79. But Thomas knows that this is not the time for the highly complex figure, for anger generates plain speaking: as Brengain herself says at l.291, 'Ne larai, Ysolt, nel vus die'. The girl's agitation at this point is indicated, at l.232, by the way her speech begins, exceptionally, with the second line of a rhyming couplet. She employs a colourful, down-to-earth image, a proverbial expression, at ll.247-48 (she will employ a proverb again, at ll.374-76, when she goes on to visit King Mark). In an earlier exchange, at ll.30-33, she develops a nice line in irony: Iseut, she feels, has hardly shown 'franchise' and yielding to Kaherdin has certainly not brought her 'honor'! Sarcasm is another weapon in her armoury, brought to bear when she openly accuses Iseut of acting as a procuress:

> Ore me dites, reïne Ysolt,
> Des quant avez esté Richolt?
> U apreïstes sun mester
> De malveis hume si apreiser
> E de une caitive traïr?

> (D., ll.54-58)

Iseut is also made to speak in a much more natural manner in this passage. She is rightly cautious, uncertain how to react, carefully picking up the key words in Brengain's utterances and repeating them:

> Ysolt respunt: 'Merci, amie!
> Unques ne vus fiz felunie;
> Ne par mal ne par malveisté
> Ne fud uncs cest plai enginné.'
>
> (D., ll.158-61)

'Felunie' echoes 'Fel' of l.134, 'malveisté' echoes the 'malvesté' of l.149 and 'enginné' Brengain's use of the same word in l.148 (note also 'engin' in l.157). This may perhaps be a little mechanical, but it is not overwhelmingly artificial. Similarly, in ll.211-16, Iseut produces essentially the same thought three times (*interpretatio*), that Mark will continue to love her whatever she may do. Thomas could have introduced here a set of three rigorously parallel couplets, but chooses instead to vary his expression in a more informal and, indeed, more natural way. Eventually Iseut's control snaps and, in her final speech which begins at l.301, she holds Brengain responsible for the way she may have behaved. But Thomas's control remains: key words of earlier speeches, 'malvesté' (l.307) and 'engin' (ll.320 and 323, note also 'enginz' in l.313) are deliberately introduced once more.

But in other circumstances where words are made to recur, the effect may not be quite so successful. The marriage episode of the first Sneyd fragment abounds in abstract terms, the meaning of which is blurred since they are employed in a variety of contexts with, apparently, slightly different shades of meaning. Consider, for example, the terms *voleir* and *desir* which figure frequently in the episode and which are closely associated in the following passages:

> Sis corages mue sovent,
> E pense molt diversement
> Cum changer puisse sun voleir,
> Quant sun desir ne puit aveir.
>
> (Sn.[1], ll.1-4)

Pur le nun e pur la belté
Que Tristrans i ad trové
Chiet en desir e en voleir
Que la meschine volt aveir.

(Sn.[1], ll.229-32)

Les dames faire le solent,
Laissent ço q'unt pur ço que volent
E asaient cum poent venir
A lor voleir, a lor desir.
Ne sai, certes, que jo en die:
Mais trop par aiment novelerie
Homes e femmes ensement,
Car trop par changent lor talent
E lor desir e lor voleir
Cuntre raisun, cuntre poeir.

(Sn.[1], ll.287-96)

Dunt me vient ceste volenté
E cest desir e cest voleir
U la force u le poeir
Que jo vers ceste m'acointai
U que jo unques l'espusai
Contre l'amur, cuntre la fei
Qu'a Ysolt m'amie dei?

(Sn.[1], ll.548-54)

Le desir qu'il ad vers la reïne
Tolt le voleir vers la meschine;
Le desir lui tolt le voleir,
Que nature n'i ad poeir.
Amur e raisun le destraint,
E le voleir de sun cors vaint.
Le grant amor qu'ad vers Ysolt
Tolt ço que la nature volt,
E vaint icele volenté
Que senz desir out en pensé.
Il out boen voleir de li faire
Mais l'amur le fait molt retraire.

> Gente la sout, bele la set
> E volt sun buen, sun desir het;
> Car s'il nen oüst si grant desir,
> A son voleir poüst asentir;
> Mais a sun grant desir asent.
>
> (Sn.[1], ll.597-613)

The problems begin with ll.1-4. As I have indicated already, in the monologue that follows Tristan will be trying to persuade himself that it is right for him to marry Iseut aux Blanches Mains. What Thomas seems to be saying as he introduces this speech is that, since Tristan realizes that he cannot profit from his love for the queen, 'sun desir', he tries to justify his firm resolve, 'sun voleir', to marry the second Iseut and seek sexual fulfilment with her. He is endeavouring to 'changer...sun voleir', to render his decision to marry Iseut more acceptable in his own eyes, to delude himself into believing that the course of action on which he is plainly set is an honourable one. But Thomas does not consistently maintain the contrast between *desir* and *voleir* he is apparently suggesting here. At l.231, part of Thomas's commentary on the monologue, we are perhaps meant to understand that Tristan has succeeded in reconciling his decision to marry the second Iseut with his love for the queen: his *voleir* and his *desir* have been made to coincide. But it is much easier to take *desir* in a less specific sense, to assume that it means much the same as *voleir* must mean here, namely 'wish, intention, resolve'. Elsewhere, it may be noted, at l.101 of Tristan's monologue, *desir* seems to have yet another sense, 'sexual satisfaction'. When *desir* and *voleir* are again associated in the text, in ll.287-96, they once more appear to be roughly synonymous and, linked as they both are with *talent* in ll.294-95, must both mean 'wish' or 'desire', people's general longing for something other than what they have. On their next joint appearance, in ll.548-54, *desir* and *voleir* once again seem to complement each other in sense: in l.549, *desir* must mean 'wish', *voleir* 'resolve' or 'will-power'. But in ll.597-613, the two terms are contrasted, *desir* being Tristan's love for the queen, *voleir* being his resolve, in this instance, to consummate his marriage to her namesake. *Desir* is clearly a superior emotion, equivalent to 'La grant amor qu'ad vers Ysolt' of l.603, and it is this *desir* which finally overcomes his *voleir*. In a consideration of this passage, Bédier wrote: '*Desir* peut en somme se traduire par *amour* au sens plein du mot, *voleir* par *concupiscence charnelle*' (*1*, vol.I, p.287, note). Undoubtedly, the form that Tristan's *voleir* takes in this particular passage is physical desire, a resolve to have carnal knowledge of his wife, spelt out in l.602 as 'le voleir de sun cors'. But it is worth pointing out that, in the whole marriage sequence, just as *desir* cannot be restricted to a single, unequivocal meaning, so *voleir* presents a range of meanings which only the context can help to define accurately.

All this does not make things exactly easy for the reader. One can only sympathize with Jodogne when he writes: 'Je concède que, traitant un sujet délicat, Thomas doit recourir aux euphémismes; mais il nous perd lorsque, voulant les opposer ci et là, il oublie ailleurs les sens qu'il leur a accordés' (*29*, p.105). Even Frappier, who is generally more confident in his pronouncements, is forced to admit: 'On sent que Thomas travaille, avec un demi-succès seulement, à créer ou à préciser son vocabulaire psychologique' (*22*, p.175, note 46). In truth, this situation may have arisen because Thomas seems very much concerned here with matters of style. In l.610, for example, Thomas introduces isocolon, two clauses of equal length, presents antitheses between *buen* and *desir* and between *volt* and *het* and arranges these antithetical ideas in a chiasmus. Elsewhere in the passages cited, he employs *annominatio* (or *traductio*) as he plays on *voleir* and its associated forms and repeats words for emphasis. But in creating stylistic effects, it is possible to neglect meaning.

Thomas's use of the same abstract terms on a number of occasions may serve to remind us that repetition, of various kinds, is a predominant feature of his style. In the marriage episode itself, we find a kind of chiastic *interpretatio*, where the words of a line are repeated after a short interval and in a different order:

Se mun desir ne puis aveir

(Sn.[1], l.62)

> S'aveir ne puis mun desir
>
> (Sn.[1], 1.67)

We also find the content of a whole couplet essentially repeated in the next. In this example of *interpretatio*, there is also a complex pattern of chiasmus:

> Tant se deit deliter al rei
> Oblier deit l'amur de mei,
> En sun seignur tant deliter
> Que sun ami deit oblier.
>
> (Sn.[1], ll.103-06)

Simliar stylistic features are found in other parts of the poem. In the first Turin fragment, Thomas intervenes in the text and introduces a couplet which is repeated, with variation, together with an introduction, after a brief interval:

> La parole mettrai avant,
> Le jugement facent amant,
> Al quel estoit mieuz de l'amor
> Ou sanz lui ait greignor dolur.
>
> (T.[1], ll.148-51)

> Ore puet qui set esgart dire
> A quel de l'amor mieuz estoit,
> Ou qui greignor dolur en ait.
>
> (T.[1], ll.181-83)

In the Douce fragment as well, we find instances of repetition, notably in ll.1258-68. In the first three lines of this passage, a thought is put forward:

> Quanque m'ad fait poi me valdra
> S'al besuingn ne me volt aider,
> Cuntre cel dolur conseiler.
>
> (D.[1], ll.1258-60)

Thomas then reiterates this thought in each of the four couplets that follow, *interpretatio* yet again, employing in each couplet part of the verb *valoir* (*annominatio*) and introducing punning word-play (*paronomasia*) on forms close if not exactly the same in sound, *valt*, *falt* and *volt*.

In these lines the repetition can be fairly easily justified, for Tristan is desperate at this point to convince Kaherdin of the importance of his mission. But elsewhere one may feel that repetition is little more than an artistic flourish, an attempt by the author to show off. For the style of Thomas is a very overt, self-conscious style. Of no writer can it more truly be said that he wears his art on his sleeve. And certainly we are constantly being reminded of the presence of our author. When Thomas inserts a detail into a digression, he employs the first person: 'A la matire n'afirt mie,/Nequedent boen est quel vos die' (Sn.[1], ll.729-30). When he ends his consideration of *ire*, he does the same thing: 'Mais jo ne os mun ben dire/Car il n'affirt nient a mei' (D., ll.1334-35). Here — contrary to the evidence — Thomas claims that he has not said all that he would like to have said on the subject. Elsewhere, as at ll.148-51 and at 181-83 of the first Turin fragment, he seems more sincere when he proposes that others, and not himself, should assess the plight of his various characters. But one still senses in his make-up a strong didactic element, which reveals itself in his discussions on *ire* and *envie*, in the commentaries he includes and in the occasional proverbial expression he inserts. He may not always commit himself, but he remains a didactic writer in that he is inviting judgment on the evidence he has personally marshalled. He may not consistently conclude himself, but he seems to be asking the reader to do so.

5. Conclusion

Conclusions are always difficult, especially when, as with our text, the evidence on which to base a conclusion is barely adequate. It is worth pointing out again that, of Thomas's complete romance, only fragments are known and, of these fragments, some are lost or destroyed. The Douce fragment is admittedly almost two thousand lines long, but even this must represent only a small proportion of the full romance. And yet, when all this has been said, common sense decrees that any final evaluation we make must be based squarely on the material that survives rather than on the many thousands of lines that are missing: to do otherwise is to indulge in idle speculation.

Unfortunately, even the material that we do have is not always very helpful. Thomas closes his romance with a brief epilogue (Sn.[2], ll.820-39), but the statement of intent which it contains proves to be not altogether clear. It is, of course, dangerous to take any declaration of this kind at its face value: the writer's own view of his work is not always consonant with our perception of it. Moreover, an epilogue can serve as the artistic equivalent of a death-bed conversion, where the poet seeks to apologize for earlier audacities. One thing, though, we can confidently assert: Thomas began his romance with a prologue:

> [E dit ai] tute la verur
> [Si cum] jo pramis al primur.
>
> (Sn.[2], ll.828-29)[8]

This prologue was presumably nothing like as substantial as Gottfried's preface of two hundred and forty-four lines, but it must have been a personal introduction to the work to come.

[8] At l.828, in spite of Wind's reservations (5, p.162), *dit ai* is still just about legible in the manuscript, but the other doubtful letters in ll.825-29 cannot now be confirmed.

After this, the difficulties arise. To whom precisely does Thomas
address himself here?

> Tumas fine ci sun escrit:
> A tuz amanz saluz i dit,
> As pensis e as amerus,
> As emvius, as desirus,
> As enveisiez e as purvers,
> [A tuz cels] ki orunt ces vers.

(Sn.[2], ll.820-25)

The sense of l.821 must be that Thomas is calling on all lovers,
without exception. Gottfried may have appealed in his prologue
to a select group of *edele herzen*, 'noble hearts', but there is no
compelling reason to suppose that Thomas has such a narrow
audience in mind. Lines 822-24 then seem to introduce the
various categories of *amanz*, presented in pairs of com-
plementary words, in sets of near-synonyms. At the close of the
epilogue the reverse process is employed: ll.837-38 present the
various kinds of related dangers to which lovers may be exposed,
before they are summed up in the global term of l.839, 'tuiz
engins d'amur'. In l.822 Thomas concerns himself with the
pensis and the *amerus*, words already associated with Tristan
and Iseut in the text (see D., ll.607 and 927, see also *Fo*, ll.2 and
152). Baumgartner and Wagner have suggested meanings for
these terms: '*Pensis* et *Amerus*...qualifient donc à notre avis les
"âmes sensibles", les "sentimentaux", ceux qui aiment, sans
être pour autant murés dans leur passion, ceux qui, tel Tristan,
telle Ysolt, savent compatir à toutes les souffrances jusqu'à en
mourir' (*14*, p.530). But it may not be wise to try to relate *pensis*
and *amerus* too closely to the main characters: Thomas is now
speaking in general terms to all lovers, not merely to those who
love in the same way as those depicted in the romance. Perhaps,
therefore, it is safer to go along with Hunt and take *pensis* and
amerus as meaning those who are already in love (see *27*, p.51).
The second synonymic pair, the *emvius* and the *desirus*, is more
difficult: *emvius* is not found elsewhere in the poem, while one
hesitates to define *desirus* too closely, related as it is to the elastic

desir. Is Thomas referring here to those who aspire to love, as opposed to those in the previous line who know love already? (But one wonders how these particular individuals can draw upon their own experiences in love (D., ll.834-35) if the emotion is still foreign to them.) The *enveisiez* and the *purvers* of l.824 also give pause. After dealing with those in love, with those who aspire to love, Thomas seems to address himself to those who love wrongly. As Baumgartner and Wagner point out (*14*, p.532), the most telling use of a related form is that of *emveisier* (Sn.[1], l.637), where the infinitive must mean something like 'to enjoy the pleasures of the flesh' and the *enveisiez* of the closing dedication may be taken to mean those who do not love seriously, whose only concern in love is with satisfying their sexual desire. If previous suppositions are correct, *purvers* must mean something analogous: Thomas may be referring here to those who wilfully limit themselves in love to the seeking of sexual fulfilment.

Thomas admits in l.826 that not all his readers will have found what they wanted in his text, suggesting that some will have found what he has had to say a little unpalatable. This idea is perhaps reinforced by l.830: 'E diz e vers i ai retrait'. Here, Thomas appears to be alluding to the dicta, the *sententiae*, which he has inserted into his poem and which, so he then claims, have contributed to the exemplary nature of the work:

> Pur essample issi ai fait
> Pur l'estoire embelir,
> Que as amanz deive plaisir,
> E que par lieus poissent troveir
> Choses u se puissent recorder.

(Sn.[2], ll.831-35)

He is not simply saying here that his work will provide both pleasure and profit: rather, he seems to be insisting that the instruction he has included is a source of pleasure in itself. Hunt notes that in l.835 Thomas uses *se recorder* rather than the more common *se mirer* (or *se remirer*) (*27*, p.52). The choice of vocabulary is doubtless deliberate: Thomas is hoping that lovers, in recognizing parallels between their own lives and the lives of his main characters, may come to a better understanding of their behaviour. Wind suggests 's'instruire' as one possible translation of *se recorder* (5, p.200) and this may well be the right meaning here. But how are lovers to draw consolation from his romance as Thomas apparently suggests in l.836? 'Aveir em poissent grant confort.' If we join the majority of critics in giving *confort* its most usual sense, in what way can this unhappy story be a means of solace?

This may be the moment to emphasize the pervading gloom of the tale told in the extant fragments. Nearly all those concerned must endure some form of suffering. In Sn.[1], Thomas shows how Tristan actually increases his own misery by marrying and brings misery to Iseut aux Blanches Mains (see ll.215-18, 471-72), while in T.[1], Thomas stresses the pain and sorrow, the 'painne e dolur' (l.72), which all his four main characters must bear. Happiness is rarely mentioned and when it is it may be its absence which is noted: 'E nuls d'aus nen i a deduit' (T.[1], l.74), 'Mais Ysolt n'en ad nul deduit' (D., l.619). Any happiness which is experienced is of very brief duration, may be tinged with sorrow or may simply be the prelude to disaster. When Tristan and Iseut are reconciled in the first section of the Douce fragment they are together for just one night (D., ll.723-26) Tristan and Kaherdin in Brittany are cheerful enough but without their ladies naturally suffer from 'ennui' (D., l.900), while the joy felt by Iseut and her companions, as their journey to France begins so well (D., ll.1539-40), soon gives way to despair, as the ship is first caught by a storm and then becalmed.

Certainly the end of the story could hardly be more sombre. The tone of the death scenes may not have been the tone of the whole text, but it is the one that remains with the modern reader and also the one that remained with the medieval public which knew the complete romance. What contributes to the darkening of the mood is the regular association of love not merely with suffering but with death. True, this idea has appeared already: the 'lai de Guiron' of Sn.[1] treats death in love and in T.[1], it will be recalled, Tristan is said to grieve for 'La bele raïne, sa amie/En cui est sa mort e sa vie' (ll.121-22), but now the references come more frequently. Tristan tells Kaherdin that the potion will bring the death of both Iseut and himself (D., ll.1223-26) and he nearly dies from 'desir' as he awaits the queen (D., l.1738). At the end, believing that life without Iseut has no purpose, Tristan elects to die at once and expires because of the love he feels for her:

> Quant a moi ne volez venir,
> Pur vostre amur m'estuet murrir.
>
> (D., ll.1761-62)

Iseut likewise is aware that she and her lover must not only suffer but die together (D., ll.1641-42) and she also nearly dies from 'desir' when her destination is in sight but still unreachable (D., l.1728). The queen recognizes as well that Tristan has indeed died because of his love for her: 'Mort estes pur la meie amur' (D., l.1813). And when Iseut lies down to die, her act of death mirrors the act of love:

> Embrace le, si s'estent,
> Baise la buche e la face
> E molt estreit a li l'enbrace,
> Cors a cors, buche a buche estent,
> Sun espirit a itant rent
> E murt dejuste lui issi
> Pur la dolur de sun ami.
>
> (Sn.[2], ll.809-15)

The manner of Iseut's death may indicate her continuing attachment to the things of the flesh. There is no sign in the text that the lovers repent in any way, no suggestion that they are about to be admitted into eternal life. When Iseut calls upon God in the storm, she is wanting Him to grant Tristan and herself a continuing existence in this world or joint oblivion:

> 'Deus nus doinst ensemble venir
> Que jo, amis, guarir vus puisse,
> U nus dous murrir d'une anguisse!'
>
> (D., ll.1692-94)

(In granting only the second of these alternatives, is God in fact *condemning* the lovers?) When Tristan dies, he asks briefly for salvation, but the bulk of his thoughts are for his lady, not for his maker (D., ll.1760-70). There is, in short, no Christian optimism to lighten the gloom of the closing lines.

What kind of consolation, then, can this blank tale possibly provide? Larmat suggests that, for lovers, being exposed to the text can be a cathartic experience:

> Pour consoler l'amoureux qui souffre, Thomas n'envisage pas de meilleur traitement que de lui raconter les 'angoisses douloureuses' de Tristan et d'Yseut, de lui découvrir leurs déchirements intimes, mais adoucis par la poésie. Le roman exerce alors la même fonction que la tragédie. Par les prestiges de l'art, il purifie la terreur et la pitié qu'il fait naître. Dû pour une part à la constatation que les plus célèbres des amants furent malheureux, le 'réconfort' viendrait surtout de l'enchantement poétique, source de la *catharsis*. (*34*, p.379)

So, lovers may be having a rough time but they can at least console themselves with the thought that Tristan and Iseut had it even rougher! But perhaps the meaning of *confort*, especially in view of its association with *encuntre*, needs to be sought elsewhere. Hunt persuasively argues that '*confort* is to be taken in its etymological sense of strengthening and together with the preposition *encuntre* indicates that lovers will find their resistance strengthened to the *engins d'amur*, which include *change*, *tort*, *paine* and *dolur*' (*27*, p.51). Certainly *confort* is frequently employed with the meaning of 'help, support'[9] and this explanation surely makes a good deal of sense. Thomas's

[9] Note especially D., ll.1631-34. In D., l.1633, *confort* must have the sense of 'help', the same sense as *aïe* in l.1630. Here, Thomas's habit of repeating much the same idea in successive groups of lines makes the meaning of *confort* transparent. See also *Amadas et Ydoine*, ed. by J.R. Reinhard (Paris, Champion, 1926), ll.4869-71: 'Assés savés qu'encontre mort/Ne puet avoir autre confort/Fors dou sousfrir, il n'i a el'.

story is emerging as a *warning* example. Lovers who have started
along the same path as Tristan and Iseut should now beat a
retreat: for those who persist, as Tristan le Nain did, the
consequences may be catastrophic.

In this study, the term 'courtly love' has been almost entirely
avoided. The term is obviously not worthless. Though critics
differ widely in their understanding of what the expression
conveys, it may be of value when one wishes to categorize
loosely a literary work. But the temptation must always be
avoided to evaluate the work on the basis of its 'courtly' or 'non-
courtly' features. Too often an author is praised because of his
assumed adherence to the so-called 'courtly code' or,
conversely, because of the way he has liberated himself from the
pretended restraints of courtly convention. Whatever name we
may care to give to the kind of love Thomas describes, he does
seem in the end to speak out against it, for all the virtuous
qualities it may inspire. Tristan dies because he loses faith in the
queen and believes she is not coming to save him, while Iseut is
so devoted to her lover that she chooses to die as well. What
Thomas seems to be saying is that to place faith in love above all
else may well lead to disillusion and disaster.

6. The 'Folie Tristan d'Oxford'

The reader already acquainted with Thomas's poem will feel on familiar ground when he comes to the *Folie Tristan d'Oxford* (*Fo*). As he reads of Tristan's decision to travel without Kaherdin to England, of the hero's adventures in disguise and of the happy outcome when the queen apparently grants him the consolation needed to save him from death, he may well remember a specific passage in the Douce fragment (l.492 ff.). There, Tristan decides to visit Iseut alone and returns to court disguised as a leper; after a number of setbacks, Tristan is eventually reconciled with Iseut and they share a brief moment of pleasure. One cannot be certain, but it may be that Thomas is continuing in a much modified form a *Folie* episode he found in his source and that the *Folie Tristan d'Oxford* is appreciably closer to the original version. That there was a *Folie* episode in the lost common source is further suggested by the presence of the episode in another full romance, in Eilhart's work, where it occurs at roughly the same point in the story (ll.8629-9032) as the leper episode in *T* and in a similar contextual setting. The tale is also found in the French Prose Romance (see *1*, vol. II, pp.374-79). However, it appears in only one late manuscript and, therefore, it may not have come directly from the common source. Certainly the account closest to the *Folie Tristan d'Oxford* is that of the *Folie Tristan de Berne* (Fb).[10] It does seem that there was a fashion for writing short, episodic works, which could be loosely attached to a certain stage in the Tristan story: Marie de France's *Chevrefoil* is an obvious case in point and shares a number of features with the *Folie* poems.

But can we be more precise about the relationship between these various retellings of the same adventure? Eilhart's version seems easy enough to assess, for it appears to be an independent

[10] For a presentation of similarities between the two *Folies*, see the appendix to this study. References to *Fb* are to the Payen edition (*51*).

development of the account in the common source, with some scenes being lengthened and others abbreviated, and with a change in emphasis. It may also, incidentally, explain the puzzling existence of a 'nevu' for Tristan at l.727 of D. (if we can accept the text). In *O*, the son of Tristan's sister suggests the hero should disguise himself. We must assume, I think, that Thomas was familiar with the kind of story told by *O*, that he was modifying the version of the common source, but failed to remember that a nephew had not previously played a role in his own, refashioned account. The relationship between *Fo* and *Fb* (and the associated relationship between *Fo* and *T*) is more problematical. In his edition of the two *Folies*, Bédier pointed out very plainly that *Fb* reflected knowledge of the material in Beroul's poem, while *Fo* reflected knowledge of *T* (see *49*, pp.vi-vii), but he was otherwise generally non-committal. He envisaged the possibility that one poem had imitated the other, or that they were both independent derivatives of a lost poem. Bédier's first hypothesis has now gained the day, largely thanks to the efforts of Hoepffner, who claimed in his editions of the *Folies* that *Fb* was written first, followed and imitated by *Fo*, which incorporated material drawn from Thomas (see *50*, pp.1-7).

Since the author of *Fo* has chosen to refurbish an already existing account (whether this was a lost version or *Fb* is ultimately unimportant), he has not left himself enormous scope for originality. He must tell of the journey to Cornwall and of the arrival of Tristan at court. He must then describe the public performance of the 'fool' in the palace and have his hero introduce the first allusions to previous events in his life: these allusions must necessarily be conventional, for they must be recognizable in order to have any impact. He must then go on to describe Tristan's private interview with Iseut, his reception by the dog and the queen's eventual acknowledgement that he is, indeed, the person he claims to be. Nevertheless, by adding material of his own invention and by drawing upon Thomas's version, the author of *Fo* has succeeded in producing a distinctive work.

The opening passage, for example, brings to mind Thomas's poem in a way no other account does. The hero is separated from Queen Iseut and is presumably living in Brittany ('sun païs', l.1), where he has been for a large part of the Thomas fragments. Tristan is in customary mood, for at l.2 he is described as 'Dolent, mornes, tristes, pensifs'. In l.13, he is said to be overwhelmed by 'Peine, dolur, penser, ahan', another set of generally familiar synonyms. We find also a characteristic association between love and death, for Tristan will not recover from the affliction presently laying him low unless he receives 'confort' (ll.5-6, 15-16): a continuing absence of love, a continuing separation from Iseut, will inevitably bring about his death (ll.17-19). One is reminded of Tristan's instructions to Kaherdin as he lies dying from his poisoned wound (see especially D., ll.1209-10). But the author does not concentrate solely on the hero's individual psychology. Just as Thomas did in his excursuses on *ire* and *envie*, he departs from the particular in ll.37-40 and enunciates a general axiom. He does the same thing in the closing lines of the exposition, ll.47-56, where he moves from a consideration of Tristan's attitudes to a statement about human behaviour in general.

As the story progresses, we find a mixture of the familiar and the unusual. Early the very next day, Tristan sets out, makes his way straight to the sea and finds a ship destined for England. A conventional description of the sailors' activities then follows: the evidence of D., ll.1317-18, suggests that the rhyme 'treff: nef' of ll.71-72 is difficult to avoid. The crossing is described in an equally unexciting manner and recalls Kaherdin's voyage to London in Thomas's poem (D., ll.1304-08, 1317-22). By contrast, the dialogue between Tristan and the sailors as he persuades them to take him with them is surprisingly lively and perhaps contains an interesting play on words. In l.78, the sailors' *a joie* seems to mean 'cheerfully' or 'with luck', but in Tristan's response in l.80—'A joie i pussez vus aler!'—the phrase may mean rather more. Is Tristan thinking of Iseut, his 'amur', his 'joie' of l.18? The same mixture of the familiar and the unexpected appears in the description of Tintagel. Its physical appearance seems inspired by other romances (see *50*, pp.16-18), but no other *Folie* story has any sustained description at all. Moreover, the author leaves his written sources and includes a detail drawn, so he claims, from oral tradition: Tintagel was once known as the Enchanted Castle, 'li chastel faez' (l.130), and disappeared twice a year. This is a pleasant enough addition to the text, but it has no influence upon the way the story develops.

At the beginning of the text Tristan had been faced with a problem, his separation from Iseut: he responded by deciding to travel to England and then put his plan into action. Whereas this narrative pattern of problem, reaction and action occurs only once in *Fb*—for Tristan's decision to 'play the fool' is made there before he leaves his homeland—the pattern is now repeated in *Fo*. In the Oxford version, Tristan is faced with the problem of getting in touch with Iseut (compare ll.3 and 155), he decides to don the guise of a fool and he is now about to act on this decision. Tristan has another good-natured encounter (found only in *Fo*) with the seafaring community, for he exchanges clothes with a passing fisherman who can hardly believe his luck. But Tristan still has to transform himself into the fool. Now he just happens to have on his person a pair of scissors, which he always carries with him since they were a gift from Iseut. In the Douce fragment, Tristan takes a goblet with him, a rather more likely gift from Iseut, but in the *Folie* Tristan must hack his hair off with something, so a pair of scissors is what he has to have. He changes his voice, a feature which will have an important part to play in the dénouement of the tale and which again is not found in any other version. Tristan then blackens his face, picks a staff from a convenient hedge and sets off for the castle. Only now in *Fo* are the external signs of Tristan's madness complete. It is worth pointing out, as Jacqueline Schaefer has done (see *55*), that Tristan is possessed by another, finer form of madness; he is mad with love for Iseut: 'Pur vostre amur sui afolez' (l.173).

On his arrival at the castle, Tristan has to convince the porter who receives him of his insanity. To do so, he speaks of the bizarre wedding of the 'abé de Munt' (l.228), which he claims to have attended. Little of this is found elsewhere: there is a porter in the Douce fragment, but he plays a different role, while in *Fb* and in *O* Tristan enters directly into Mark's presence. The author of *Fo* has chosen to embellish the tale and to use the porter to give the hero in his new guise his first test. There is more light-hearted banter when Tristan, after being admitted to the palace, responds to Mark's questioning. This is a scene found in all versions but always with certain individual characteristics. Tristan claims his mother was a whale and that he was reared by a tigress; he offers to give Mark his sister in exchange for Iseut, whom he is proposing to carry off to his crystal dwelling suspended in the air. I suppose the fool's words invite interpretation: the whale recalls the hero's birth at sea, the tigress his difficult childhood and the palace of glass his impossible dreams of a refuge away from the trials of the real world (see *54*). But what counts is the effect of the fool's words, the relaxed, unwatchful mood he is creating amongst his listeners. However, when he introduces his first reference to his past life and claims to be 'Trantris', the effect his words have upon Iseut is quite different:

> Ysolt, l'entent, del quer suspire.
> Vers le fol ad curuz e ire.

(ll.317-18)

As Tristan goes on to develop this first, brief allusion and to introduce others, the poem almost changes its nature. The progress of the tale itself comes to a virtual halt as Tristan begins to reconstruct the story of his life, according to the version produced by Thomas. In a way, this change is announced in advance: the porter called Tristan the 'fis Urgan le velu' (l.242), referring to a giant killed by Tristan himself in Thomas's version of the legend (see *1*, vol.I, pp.219-24), and the audience has thus been prepared for the more substantial references that now come. Whereas the order of the allusions made in *Fb* is fairly haphazard, the author of *Fo* seems to have made a conscious decision to retell events roughly in the order in which they occurred. Tristan speaks of the Morholt, of his first stay in Ireland and of his second journey to that country in search of Iseut. His account is regularly punctuated by similar phrases—'Membrer vus dait' (ll.327, 361, see also l.415), 'Ne

vus menbre' (1.389), 'Ne menbre vus' (1.461)—which further
mark these passages off from anything that has gone before.
One has the sense here that a parallel story is being formed: the
tale of the fool is being joined by a legend, by the story of the
almost mythical exploits of Tristan. Not that the tale is
completely abandoned, for the reactions of the characters are
still recorded. The king continues to be amused, but Iseut grows
ever more uncertain. She refuses to associate this figure with
'Trantris' for he is physically so unlike him (ll.365-68). One
reference by the fool has a profoundly unsettling effect on her.
In a smooth transfer from tale to legend, Tristan is inspired by
Iseut's accusation of drunkenness to recall the time they drank
the potion together (ll.459-74). When she hears tell of this
crucial event in her life, Iseut is stunned into silence.

Tristan meanwhile must maintain his image of fool. In a
passage which is an invention on the part of the author of *Fo*, he
claims to hunt birds with dogs and to catch wild animals with
birds of prey (ll.489-512). This is obviously the kind of insane
behaviour required of the fool, and yet the passage is not devoid
of further resonance, for we remember Tristan's reputation as a
mighty hunter, just as his claims to skills as a swordsman, as a
musician and especially as a lover (ll.513-26) recall the hero's
achievements in other areas: the tale, even in these apparently
casual lines, is continuing to recreate the legend.

Iseut now withdraws to her room and her emotional state is
described at some length (ll.539-48). (In *Fb*, by contrast, there is
only a very brief notation (ll.258-59).) In the conversation with
Brengain that follows, Iseut's state of mind is explored further
and her emotional disarray emphasized: 'Quant je vai, tut m'est
a contraire' (1.555).[11] As she did earlier, Iseut refuses to
countenance that the fool could be Tristan, because of his
physical dissimilarity above all (ll.575-78). Brengain's role in this
section may recall the part she played in *T*, for ll.589-92 may
bring back to mind her rebuke of the queen at the beginning of
the Douce fragment (compare especially 1.591 of *Fo* and 1.56 of
D.), but there is gentle chiding here rather than fierce sarcasm.

---

[11] Contrary to what Payen indicates in his translation (*51*, p.282), *vai* in 1.555
must be a part of *voir* rather than of *aller*.

Brengain is sent by Iseut to interrogate the fool. Attempting to convince her of his identity, Tristan picks up where he left off in the retelling of his life story, for he mentions again the drinking of the potion at sea. This is obviously an appropriate event to recall, for Brengain was herself involved and, as Tristan points out (ll.663-64), it was known only to a very few. Phrases familiar from the previous set of allusions return ('ne vus menbre' (l.624), 'Membrer vus dait' (l.632)) and again mark off this passage from the normal narrative tale. In this scene, Tristan seems to become increasingly more desperate, behaviour which may be held to contrast with his attitude elsewhere (see *52*, p.8), but in order to gain access to Iseut Tristan knows he must persuade Brengain that he is who he says he is. Not that it is ever made clear in *Fo* that Brengain is so persuaded, but her actions in l.665 ff. suggest this. And, of course, it is Iseut above all others whom Tristan must convince and upon whom attention will rightly be focused.

The final scene begins, in fact, with a fairly full indication of the moods of both Iseut and Tristan. In *Fb*, at this same point (ll.335-37), the queen's straightforward animosity is briefly recorded, but in *Fo* her reactions are more complex. She withdraws instinctively when Tristan goes to kiss her and is quite embarrassed, not knowing at all what to do. Tristan likewise retreats, taken aback at her rejection (ll.677-86). He then recovers somewhat and reproaches her with forgetfulness (ll.687-706), but Iseut once again finds that the physical appearance of this man rules out any possible identification with her lover:

> Ysolt respunt: 'Frere, ne sai.
> E vus esguard e si m'esmai,
> Kar n'aperceif mie de vus
> Ke seiez Tristran l'amerus.'
>
> (ll.707-10)

'Tristran l'amerus', significantly, seems to be a term borrowed from Thomas (see D., ll.927, 1014).

Tristan now embarks upon another set of allusions, referring to episodes related (if not exclusively) in *T*. Once more we find the characteristic phrases, 'Ne vus membre' (l.713), 'vus redait ben menbrer' (l.725) etc. This is a long section, running for well over a hundred lines until Iseut's response is reported in l.835: the tale is surrendering, albeit temporarily, to the legend. This time, the episodes are not recalled in any strictly chronological order, yet one still has a sense of deliberate arrangement. To begin, Tristan refers to the Mariadoc affair (see *1*, vol.I, pp.175-82): the seneschal was, as the hero stresses (ll.723-24) the first person to accuse them. One might expect that Tristan would now recall the attempts to ensnare the lovers that immediately followed, but in fact he moves on in time and mentions a second enemy of the lovers, the dwarf, and the main incident in which he was involved (ll.725-54). In Thomas's version, what came next was Iseut's ambiguous oath, but the author of *Fo* perhaps feels the time has come for Tristan to recall less traumatic experiences. Accordingly, he now mentions the Petitcrû episode (see *1*, vol.I, pp.217-31) and the earlier 'Harpe et rote' incident (see *1*, vol.I, pp.168-75), which, although with an unpleasant beginning for the queen, had an undeniably happy ending (ll.755-74). He then goes on to recall the Tryst episode at some length (ll.775-814) and then finally the queen's ambiguous oath (ll.815-32).

Iseut still refuses to recognize in this shambling wreck the Tristan she loves:

> Kar Tristran ne semblout il pas
> De vis, de semblanz ne de dras.

(ll.837-38)

So Tristan must try yet again and refers now to their life together in the forest (ll.855-92). This is a popular episode found in all versions, but the author of *Fo* has chosen to follow Thomas's account (see *1*, vol.I, pp.231-47). As in *T*, the lovers are presented as having left court together and their home in the forest is a hollowed-out rock. It is strange, however, to find the dwarf mentioned as active at this time: this may be nothing more than a temporary aberration on our author's part.

The tale is apparently building towards a climax. The dog, Husdent, has been remembered a moment ago (l.871) and now Tristan asks for it to be produced. It is nowhere recorded in *T* that Tristan gave the dog to the queen, but our author seems to have accepted that the appearance of the dog is an indispensable part of any *Folie* tale. His submission to his source in this respect emerges clearly when Husdent recognizes and delightedly greets his master, for ll.913-16 of *Fo* could hardly be closer to ll.514-16 of *Fb*. But even in the light of this evidence, Iseut remains uncertain. As he has done already (ll.852-54), Tristan questions her loyalty (ll.935-40) and then recalls the moment when they parted in the garden. This is a scene found only in Thomas's version and, naturally enough, it is only in *Fo* of the *Folie* tales that allusion is made to it. This final, concluding reference to the legend is an appropriate one, for the *Verger* scene is the most recent one to be evoked. Iseut still demands more, the material evidence of the ring she entrusted to Tristan on that occasion:

> Isolt dit: 'Les ensengnez crei.
> Avez l'anel? Mustrez le mei.'
>
> (ll.955-56)

With the production of the ring in the Berne *Folie* the tale is as good as over. The ring and the Homeric hound do their work and convince Iseut that Tristan really does stand before her (*Fb*, ll.540-44). But the author of *Fo* has one last trick up his sleeve. When Tristan gives her the ring, instead of bewailing her failure to recognize him as she does in *Fb*, Iseut presumes that Tristan is dead:

> 'Lasse, fet ele, mar nasqui!
> En fin ai perdu mun ami,
> Kar ço sai je ben, s'il vif fust,
> Kë autre hum cest anel n'eüst.
>
> (ll.961-64)

In face of her distress and her now obvious devotion, Tristan speaks in his true voice and with this change in his physical

nature—although the dog had little difficulty recognizing his
assumed voice earlier!—Iseut finally acknowledges that he is
indeed her lover. A few, brief moments of happiness lie before
them.

Stylistically, the Oxford *Folie* shares a number of features
with *T*. One or two of these present in the opening section have
been touched upon already, but it is worth mentioning others. In
the very first lines, a set of rhyme-words is repeated, namely
'guarir: murir', in ll.5-6 and in ll.15-16. As in Thomas's version,
this form of repetition reinforces a basic theme of the passage, in
this case the inevitability of death unless Tristan finds some
consolation. Another kind of repetition is found in ll.7-10,
where the author introduces *interpretatio* and essentially
rewrites the content of one couplet in the next:

> Melz volt murir a une faiz
> Ke tuz dis estre si destraiz,
> E melz volt une faiz murir
> Ke tuz tens en poine languir.

This device is again familiar from Thomas and is found
elsewhere in *Fo*, in ll.37-40, in ll.215-18 and ll.423-26, for
example. The extent to which material is repeated in these
instances tends to vary: sometimes material is taken over almost
wholesale, while on other occasions it is the basic idea, rather
than the precise form of words, which is reiterated in the second
couplet. There can also be small-scale repetition, of words or
phrases, rather than of full couplets. *Anaphora* is found in
ll.169-72, whilst ll.275-77 present an example of *anadiplosis*, a
form of repetition serving to link two successive clauses (see also
ll.4-7):

> Ysolt, pur vus tant par me doil!
> Ysolt, pur vus ben murir voil.
> Ysolt, se ci me savïez
> Ne sai s'a mai parlerïez.

(ll.169-72)

> Un grant tigre m'aleitat
> En une roche u me truvat.
> El me truvat suz un perun.
>
> (ll.275-77)

Repetition may be a fairly simple technique, but it is at least a conscious device, one which reveals a degree of stylistic awareness presumably instilled originally in rhetoric classes. But there are cases in *Fo*, exactly as there are in *T*, where the writing is relatively slipshod. It does not seem that a great deal of attention was lavished on the brief narrative passage at the end of the first scene in the palace (ll.531-38); l.536—'Cum a costume faire solt'—seems something of a 'filler' line, and the same might be said of l.538. The description of Tintagel is introduced by some adequate, but unexceptional lines:

> Li roi Markes i surjurnout,
> Si fesait la reïne Ysolt,
> E la grant curt iloc esteit
> Cum li reis a custume aveit.
>
> (ll.95-98)

At the end of the description of the castle, the author must return to his narrative and he seems satisfied to repeat material rather than introduce real variety (note the rhymes of ll.97-98 and ll.145-46):

> Nuveles demande e enquert
> Del rai Markes e u il ert.
> Hom li dit k'en la vile esteit
> E grant curt tenuë aveit.
>
> (ll.143-46)

One could argue that the author is deliberately trying to 'frame' the passage and to indicate clearly what he himself has invented. Be that as it may, the Tintagel passage stands out far more strongly as an almost gratuitous interpolation than it need have done. Certainly there are moments when the author exercises much greater care and control. In ll.699-706, an image is introduced and cleverly sustained, while in ll.177-86 the author plays effectively with an apparent paradox, that in adopting the disguise of a fool Tristan is acting in an extremely shrewd manner. But perhaps in this last case our author goes on for too long: ll.181-82 repeat the thought of l.180, ll.185-86 the thought and the construction of ll.183-84. On occasion, Thomas may exhibit the same tendency (the whole of this passage in *Fo* could, in fact, have been inspired by ll.564-65 of D.). At the end of his study of stylistic features in *Fo* and *T*, Hoepffner claimed: 'Bref, où que l'on regarde, les deux auteurs se ressemblent singulièrement' (*50*, p.34). This may be an exaggeration, for while the author of *Fo* uses some devices, notably *anadiplosis*, perhaps more often than Thomas, he is generally less steeped in rhetoric. Nevertheless, one can still say that the *Folie* is strongly reminiscent of Thomas's version 'par le style, par le tour et le ton' (see *49*, p.3).

A similar close association between the two texts in the way the lovers' relationship is presented might seem at first sight ruled out: where the romance ends tragically, the tale ends happily. Yet all the signs are that this happiness will be of short duration and that Tristan and Iseut will not be together for long: l.990 suggests that after one night the lovers will be forced to separate. Moreover, we are made aware that the general tenor of their lives is governed by the drinking of the love potion, presented by Tristan as producing misfortune:

> Ivrë ai esté tut tens puis,
> Mais *male* ivrece mult i truis.
>
> (ll.473-74)

> Cel baivre, bele, *mar* le bui,
> E jë unques *mar* vus conui.
>
> (ll.655-56)

We have seen that in Thomas's romance drinking the potion is also associated with misfortune and, indeed, with death (see D., ll.1223-26).

There are other aspects of the lovers' relationship in the episodic tale which recall their relationship in the romance. We are made aware, for example, of the lovers' emotional parity. At the start, separated from Iseut, Tristan is said to be 'Dolent, mornes, tristes, pensifs' (l.2). When he lands at Tintagel, he is told that Iseut is, as usual, 'Pensive' (l.152) and, when she later withdraws to her room, the author then writes:

> En la chambre vent mult pensive.
> Dolente se claime e chaitive.
>
> (ll.545-46)

Sentimentally, Tristan and Iseut are as one. We are also made aware of the loyalty the lovers show to one another. One purpose of Tristan's journey is to inform Iseut that he is dying for love of her:

> Murir desiret, murir volt,
> Mais seul tant quë ele soüst
> K'il pur la sue amur murrust,
> Kar si Ysolt sa mort saveit,
> Siveus plus suëf en murreit.
>
> (ll.20-24)

In suggesting that he would have a sweeter death if he knew Iseut was aware he was dying, Tristan echoes the queen's feelings when caught in the storm on her way to Brittany in *T*:

> Tristran, s'a vus parlé eüsse,
> Ne me calsist se puis morusse.
> Beals amis, quant orét ma mort,
> Ben sai puis n'avrez ja confort.
>
> (D., ll.1619-22)

Iseut is assuming here that Tristan would not live much longer once he knew of her death and is finding solace in the thought of their joint departure from this life. Although ll.20-24 do not make it clear, it does seem that in the *Folie* Tristan is assuming the same thing, that once his partner knew he had expired she would soon perish as well, that her loyalty would extend even unto death. At the end of the tale, Iseut's reaction is precisely the one Tristan may be predicting in the opening lines, for when she believes her lover is dead, she is quite inconsolable:

> Mais or sai jo ben k'il est mort.
> Lasse! ja mais n'avrai confort!
>
> (ll.965-66)

The author's desire to show the lovers' loyalty to each other may explain the shift of emphasis one senses in the text. At first, Tristan is trying to prove he is the person he claims to be, but his attempt falls flat: his references back fail to convince Iseut and even his reception by the dog does not persuade her. He could then revert at once to his natural voice, but he opts instead to test her. Only when he is convinced of her devotion, when she proves she is the person she always was, does he drop all pretence:

> Puis li ad dit: 'Dame raïne,
> Bele estes vus e enterine.
> Dès or ne m'en voil mès cuvrir,
> Cunuistre me frai e oïr.'
>
> (ll.969-72)

I suppose we should not be surprised by these similarities in style and content, for the author of *Fo* has shown his dependence upon Thomas's version of the story when he recreated the legend within his episodic tale. But perhaps it is the interaction of legend and tale which should be emphasized. The author of the *Folie* draws on the legend for the substance of his work and the lovers respond to each other for this brief span of time as they respond to each other in the full romance: the legend informs the tale, the tale illustrates the legend.

Appendix

Below are listed themes which appear in both the *Folie de Berne* and the *Folie d'Oxford*. References are given to the Payen edition, as it is more accessible to students, although the Hoepffner editions are still the standard texts and references to them are given in brackets. This appendix first appeared in the study by Peter S. Noble, *Beroul's 'Tristan' and the 'Folie de Berne'* (London, Grant and Cutler, 1982).

MAIN PARALLELS: SHARED ALLUSIONS TO PAST EVENTS

Berne		Oxford
	Tristan plays harp	
397-400		351-54, 359-60
(395-97)		(353-56, 361-62)
	Curing of wound inflicted by Morholt	
401-05		350, 355-58, 361-62
(399-402)		(352, 357-60, 363-64)
	Curing of wound received from dragon	
406-08		414-26
(404-06)		(416-28)
	Tristan's bath when Iseut recognizes the damaged sword	
409-20		427-44
(407-18)		(429-46)
	Departure from Ireland	
426-27		461-64, 624-40
(424-25)		(463-66, 626-42)
	Drinking of the love potion	
428-38		641-54
(426-36)		(643-56)
	The Irish harper incident	
380-93		761-74
(378-91)		(763-76)
	Mark's discovery of the lovers in the forest	
196-209		877-87
(194-207)		(879-90)

Bibliography

Thomas

Editions of Thomas's poem

1. Bédier, J., ed., *Le Roman de Tristan par Thomas, poème du XIIe siècle*, Volume I, Texte (Paris, Firmin-Didot, 1902), Volume II, Introduction (Paris, Firmin-Didot, 1905).
2. Michel, F., ed., *Tristan: recueil de ce qui reste des poëmes relatifs à ses aventures composés en françois, en anglo-normand et en grec dans les XII et XIII siècles*, 3 vols (London, Pickering, 1835-39), III, 83-94.
3. Novati, F., 'Un nuovo ed un vecchio frammento del *Tristran* di Tommaso', *Studj di filologia romanza*, II (1887), 396-515.
4. Wind, B.H., ed., *Les Fragments du roman de Tristan, poème du XIIe siècle* (Leiden, Brill, 1950).
5. ——*Thomas: les fragments du roman de Tristan, poème du XIIe siècle* (Geneva and Paris, Droz, 1960).

Other editions

6. Buschinger, D., ed., *Eilhart von Oberg, Tristrant* (Göppingen, Kummerle, 1976).
7. Ewert, A., ed., *The Romance of Tristran by Beroul: a poem of the twelfth century*, Volume I, Introduction, Text, Glossary, Index (Oxford, Blackwell, 1939), Volume II, Introduction, Commentary (Oxford, Blackwell, 1970).
8. Kölbing, E., ed., *Die nordische und die englische Version der Tristansage* (Heilbronn, Henninger, 1883).
9. Payen, J.C., ed., *Tristan et Yseut* (see *51*).
10. Ranke, F., ed., *Gottfried von Strassburg, Tristan und Isold*, tenth edition (Berlin, Zurich and Dublin, Weidmann, 1966).

Translations

11. Hatto, A.T., trans., *Gottfried von Strassburg, Tristan, translated entire for the first time, with the surviving fragments of the 'Tristran' of Thomas* (Harmondsworth, Penguin, 1960).
12. Thomas, J.W., trans., *Eilhart von Oberge's 'Tristrant'* (Lincoln and London, University of Nebraska Press, 1978).

Studies

13. Adams, A., 'The metaphor of *folie* in Thomas' *Tristan*', *Forum for Modern Language Studies*, XVII (1981), 88-90.
14. Baumgartner, E., and R.-L. Wagner, ' "As enveisiez e as purvers" ', *Romania*, LXXXVIII (1967), 527-37.
15. Bertolucci Pizzorusso, V., 'La retorica nel *Tristano* di Thomas', *Studi mediolatini e volgari*, VI-VII (1959), 25-61.
16. Bromiley, G.N., 'A pattern of narrative development in the early Tristan poems', *Modern Language Review*, LXX (1975), 743-51.
17. Bullock-Davies, C., *Professional Interpreters and the Matter of Britain* (Cardiff, University of Wales Press, 1966).
18. Dubois, C., 'A propos d'un vers du *Tristan* de Thomas: *Al lever que fait des chalons*', in *Mélanges de linguistique romane et de philologie médiévales offerts à M. Maurice Delbouille, I, Linguistique romane* (Gembloux, Duculot, 1964), pp.163-72.
19. Faral, E., *Les Arts poétiques du XIIe et XIIIe siècles: recherches et documents sur la technique littéraire du moyen âge* (Paris, Champion, 1924).
20. Fourrier, A., *Le Courant réaliste dans le roman courtois en France au moyen-âge, I, Les débuts (XIIe siècle)* (Paris, Nizet, 1960).
21. Frappier, J., 'Structure et sens du *Tristan*: version commune, version courtoise', *Cahiers de civilisation médiévale*, VI (1963), 255-80, 441-54.
22. ——, 'Sur le mot "raison" dans le *Tristan* de Thomas d'Angleterre', in *Linguistic and Literary Studies in Honor of Helmut A. Hatzfeld* (Washington, Catholic University of America Press, 1964), pp.163-76.
23. Gallais, P., 'Bleheri, la cour de Poitiers et la diffusion des récits arthuriens sur le continent', in *Moyen âge et littérature comparée* (Paris, Didier, 1967), pp.47-79.
24. Grisward, J., 'A propos du thème descriptif de la tempête chez Thomas d'Angleterre', in *Mélanges de langue et de littérature du moyen âge et de la Renaissance offerts à Jean Frappier*, 2 vols (Geneva, Droz, 1970), I, pp.375-89.
25. Harris, S.C., 'The cave of lovers in the "Tristramssaga" and related Tristan romances', *Romania*, XCVIII (1977), 306-30, 460-500.
26. Hilka, A., 'Der Tristanroman des Thomas und die *Disciplina clericalis*', *Zeitschrift für französische Sprache und Literatur*, XLV (1919), 38-46.
27. Hunt, T., 'The significance of Thomas's *Tristan*', *Reading Medieval Studies*, VII (1981), 41-61.
28. Jirmounsky, M.M., 'Quelques remarques sur la datation du *Tristan* de Thomas. Discussion de méthode', *Archivum Romanicum*, XI (1927), 210-22.
29. Jodogne, O., 'Comment Thomas d'Angleterre a compris l'amour de Tristan et d'Iseut', *Les Lettres Romanes*, XIX (1965), 103-19.
30. Johnson, P., '*Dolor, dolent* et *soi doloir*: le vocabulaire de la douleur et

la conception de l'amour selon Béroul et Thomas', *Romance Philology*, XXVI (1973), 546-54.

31. Jonin, P., *Les Personnages féminins dans les romans français de Tristan au XIIe siècle: étude des influences contemporaines* (Gap, Ophrys, 1958).

32. Kelly, D., '*En uni dire (Tristan* Douce 839) and the composition of Thomas's *Tristan*', *Modern Philology*, LXVII (1969-70), 9-17.

33. ——, 'Topical invention in medieval French literature', in *Medieval Eloquence: studies in the theory and practice of medieval rhetoric*, edited by J.J. Murphy (Berkeley, University of California Press, 1978), pp.231-51.

34. Larmat, J., 'La souffrance dans le *Tristan* de Thomas', in *Mélanges de langue et de littérature françaises du moyen-âge offerts à Pierre Jonin* (Sénéfiance, 7) (Aix-en-Provence, Publications du CUERMA, 1979), pp.369-85.

35. Lefay-Toury, M.-N., *La Tentation du suicide dans le roman français du XIIe siècle* (Paris, Champion, 1979).

36. Legge, M.D., 'Encore la date du *Tristan* de Thomas', *Bulletin bibliographique de la Société Internationale Arthurienne*, VI (1954), 95-96.

37. ——, *Anglo-Norman Literature and its Background* (Oxford, Clarendon Press, 1960).

38. Lejeune, R., 'Rôle littéraire d'Aliénor d'Aquitaine et sa famille', *Cultura neolatina*, XIV (1954), 5-57.

39. Luttrell, C., *The Creation of the First Arthurian Romance: a quest*, (London, Edward Arnold, 1974).

40. Pauphilet, A., *Le Legs du moyen âge: études de littérature médiévale* (Melun, Librairie d'Argences, 1950).

41. Pelan, M., *L'Influence du 'Brut' de Wace sur les romanciers français de son temps* (Paris, Droz, 1931).

42. Pensom, R., 'Rhetoric and psychology in Thomas's "Tristan" ', *Modern Language Review*, LXXVIII (1983), 285-97.

43. Polak, L., 'The two caves of love in the *Tristan* by Thomas', *Journal of the Warburg and Courtauld Institutes*, XXXIII (1970), 52-69.

44. ——, *Chrétien de Troyes: Cligés* (London, Grant and Cutler, 1982).

45. Shoaf, J.P., 'The owl dialogue in Thomas' *Tristan*', *Tristania*, IV, 1 (1978), 35-54.

46. Shirt, D.J., *The Old French Tristan Poems: a bibliographical guide* (London, Grant and Cutler, 1980).

47. Warren, F.M., 'Some features of style in early French narrative poetry (1150-70)', *Modern Philology*, III (1905-06), 179-209, 513-39; IV (1906-07), 655-75.

48. Wind, B.H., 'Nos incertitudes au sujet du "Tristan" de Thomas', in *Mélanges de langue et de littérature du moyen âge et de la Renaissance offerts à Jean Frappier*, 2 vols (Geneva, Droz, 1970), II, pp.1129-38.

Folie Tristan d'Oxford

Editions

49. Bédier, J., ed., *Les Deux poèmes de la Folie Tristan* (Paris, Firmin-Didot, 1907).
50. Hoepffner, E., ed., *La Folie Tristan d'Oxford* (Paris, Belles Lettres, 1938).
51. Payen, J.C., ed., *Tristan et Yseut: les 'Tristan' en vers, 'Tristan' de Béroul, 'Tristan' de Thomas, 'Folie Tristan' de Berne, 'Folie Tristan' d'Oxford, 'Chèvrefeuille' de Marie de France* (Paris, Garnier, 1974).

Studies

52. Curtis, R.L., 'The humble and the cruel Tristan: a new look at the two poems of the *Folie Tristan*', *Tristania*, II, 1 (1976), 3-11.
53. Haidu, P., 'Text, pretextuality and myth in the *Folie Tristan d'Oxford*', *Modern Language Notes*, LXXXVIII (1973), 712-17.
54. Payen, J.C., 'Le Palais de verre dans la *Folie d'Oxford*. De la folie métaphorique à la folie vécue, ou: le rêve de l'île déserte à l'heure de l'exil: notes sur l'érotique des *Tristan*', *Tristania*, V, 2 (1980), 17-27.
55. Schaefer, J.T., 'Tristan's folly: feigned or real?', *Tristania*, III, 1 (1977) 3-16.

CRITICAL GUIDES TO FRENCH TEXTS

edited by
Roger Little, Wolfgang van Emden, David Williams